C(
MOU
OUTD

HIKING
SAFETY
HANDBOOK

Art Hogling

COLORADO
MOUNTAIN CLUB

The Colorado Mountain Club Press
Golden, Colorado

Hiking Safety Handbook
© 2023 Art Hogling

Published by:
The Colorado Mountain Club Press
710 10th Street, Suite 200, Golden, CO 80401
(303) 996-2743 | cmcpress@cmc.org | cmc.org/books

Founded in 1912, The Colorado Mountain Club is the largest outdoor recreation, education, and conservation organization in the Rocky Mountains. Look for our books at your local bookstore or outdoor retailer, or online at cmc.org/books.

Corrections: We greatly appreciate when readers alert us to errors or outdated information by emailing cmcpress@cmc.org.

Vicki Hopewell: design and composition
Casey Blaine: editor

Front cover photo by Frank Burzynski
Back cover photo by Adam Johanknecht

Distributed to the book trade by:
Mountaineers Books
1001 SW Klickitat Way, Suite 201, Seattle, WA 98134
(800) 553-4453 | mountaineersbooks.org

We gratefully acknowledge the financial support of the people of Colorado through the Scientific and Cultural Facilities District of greater metropolitan Denver for our publishing activities.

Printed in Korea

ISBN 978-1-937052-86-7
Ebook ISBN 978-1-937052-88-1

23 24 25 / 10 9 8 7 6 5 4 3 2 1

WARNING AND DISCLAIMER
Read, Enjoy, and Proceed at your own Risk

OUTDOOR RECREATION IS HAZARDOUS AND CAN EVEN BE DANGEROUS AND LIFE-THREATENING. Weather and terrain conditions can change often, rapidly, and unpredictably. Techniques, routes, and equipment change and evolve, and in the case of equipment, can wear out or break. Participant skills, abilities, and physical conditioning can also change or be inadequate for weather and terrain. The users or readers of this and all other Colorado Mountain Club ("CMC") books, articles, videos, and websites are solely responsible for their own safety, including using common sense and fully understanding their own knowledge, skills, abilities, equipment, surroundings, and conditions, and proceed at their own risk.

The information in this and all other CMC books, articles, videos, and websites is general in nature; discrepancies may exist between the text and the trails or routes in the field. Land managers may change, alter, or close trails. Check with local land management agencies before proceeding to receive the latest information and warnings.

HIKING, BACKCOUNTRY TRAVEL, MOUNTAINEERING, ALPINE CLIMBING, BACKCOUNTRY SKIING, ROCK CLIMBING, BOULDERING, ICE CLIMBING, AND OTHER MOUNTAIN AND OUTDOOR RECREATIONAL ACTIVITIES ARE DANGEROUS AND MAY RESULT IN SEVERE AND/OR PERMANENT INJURY OR DEATH. The user of the information contained in this publication assumes all risks of the use and application of the information provided or discussed within it.

The authors and CMC expressly disclaim all liability arising out of or related to the content of this and all other CMC books, articles, videos, and websites. The authors and publishers make no representations or warranties, express or implied, of any kind regarding the contents of these publications. All representations and warranties, express or implied, regarding this and all other CMC books, articles, videos, and websites and the accuracy of the information therein and the results of the use thereof are expressly disclaimed, including but not limited to any and all warranties of Merchantability and Fitness for a Particular Purpose.

CONTENTS

"One thorn of experience is
worth a whole wilderness of warning."

—JAMES RUSSELL LOWELL
Nineteenth-century American poet and diplomat

Checking the map
Photo by Adam Johanknecht

INTRODUCTION

Wilderness travel can bring tremendous adventure and joy to life. But for the unprepared, the same backcountry experience can bring pain, fear, and in the worst-case scenario, even death. Education and experience are the key elements that keep the balance on the joy side of the equation.

Wilderness safety education has been an important value of the Colorado Mountain Club (CMC) since its founding in 1912. Decades of classes, schools, field trips, and lectures have created a safety culture that has enabled safer outdoor experiences for generations of adventurers. This handbook has its origins in those classes. The Backpacking School, Wilderness First Aid program, and Hiking Safety Seminars are where I have served as a lead instructor and school director for over twenty years. Many of the chapters here began as instructional training guides and have been continuously updated with current research and field experience.

This book also benefits from the constructive feedback of thousands of students over the years. Hiking Safety Seminar instructors are among the most experienced outdoor educators anywhere. Yet, students have repeatedly shared that they particularly value learning from the many mistakes, close calls, and authentic, real-life escapes our instructors have encountered. Thus, each chapter begins with a content-relevant scenario titled "Don't Let This Happen to You." These are all actual events, gone awry, with some modifications to names and locations.

This book also reflects several major sea changes that are occurring in the American West. One is the dramatic population growth, as many individuals choose to move here for the inspiring scenery, clean environment, and recreational opportunities. This has been facilitated by technological innovations that allow productive work in widely dispersed locations. Population growth has, in turn, led to increased backcountry visitation. Add to these trends the effect of the COVID-19 pandemic, which has brought its own, unique dynamics to what has been called the outdoor surge. The requirements for social distancing, the benefits of fresh air—coupled with closed fitness and recreation centers, ski resorts, and climbing gyms—introduced (or reintroduced) many to the physical and mental health benefits of backcountry outdoor recreation.

Across the Western US, there are now millions of new users on public lands. In many ways, this is a very good thing. For years, Yellowstone Park rangers have had a saying, "Those that visit, if even only once, will be a park supporter for life."

Busy times on the trails . . .

Wilderness advocates similarly share that it is the users of the backcountry who become its strongest defenders and supporters.

The downsides of the surge are full parking lots, crowded trails, trash, soil erosion, and stressed wildlife. New users may unknowingly venture beyond their skill level and safety knowledge. This has resulted in a dramatic increase in search and rescue (SAR) missions. Rescue teams, which are traditionally staffed by volunteers, report record numbers of emergency calls. Teams share anecdotes of burnout, overwork, fatigue, and stress injury.

A landmark, in-depth study of the situation was completed in 2022 by the Colorado Department of Parks and Wildlife (CPW). Its report found that Colorado SAR teams responded to,

. . . means busy times for search and rescue.

on average, 3,600 incidents a year, more than any other state, overwhelmingly for hikers and backpackers. It described heroic volunteer responders being pushed beyond their limits with increasing cases of physical injury and mental-health stress. The report makes many important recommendations including increased support, resources, and insurance benefits for rescue workers.

The report also makes a strong call for addressing the growing number of backcountry incidents through specific safety education for wilderness users. Researchers propose dramatically expanding a concept known as preventative search and rescue (PSAR). It was first developed by National Park Service rangers who noticed increased backcountry emergencies among national park visitors. This proactive approach encourages increased education of public land users in backcountry safety techniques, thus reducing the numbers of emergency incidents. CMC's expanding list of safety training and "outdoor skills" publications, such as this book, is, in part, a response to this critical need. My aim and hope is that *Hiking Safety Handbook* will make a meaningful contribution to PSAR education and the safety of public land users.

SAR volunteers honorably risk their lives every time they respond to a call for a backcountry mission. We backcountry users can do our part by always acknowledging personal responsibility for our individual safety. To the level of our abilities, we should work to avoid incidents and view self-rescue as our first priority. If you are reading this handbook, you recognize and share this value. You are to be commended for this effort to educate yourself in preventative safety practices. Your first steps can include committing to a personal safety philosophy as described in Chapter 1, developing a lifelong learning approach to safety education, passing these skills on to family members and hiking partners, and sharing the strength and joy you gain from the wilderness with others.

Safe trails!
—*Dr. Art Hogling (trail name "Sage")*

1

The Meaning of Safety

My wake-up call came late in the afternoon. The imaginary voice on the other end of the imaginary phone said, "You do not have the skills you need for this kind of hike. You are probably going to die."

I had to agree. Things did not look good. I had gotten off route at 13,500 feet on my solo trip of Colorado's Mount Lindsey, a trip rated easy/moderate. My rain gear had "wetted out," it was hailing hard, water gushed down the gully I was in, and the occasional rubble block whizzed past my unhelmeted head.

My sorry state did not correspond with the image I had of myself. I had hiked, backpacked, and climbed extensively in the Eastern United States, before being recruited for my dream job in the West. Since arriving, I had successfully climbed twenty fourteeners, backpacked a lot, and hiked weekly. Recently, a friend had invited me to climb Washington's Mount Rainier.

Knowing we did not have the snow-climbing skills required, we enrolled in pretrip alpine climbing classes taught by certified mountain guides both in Colorado and Washington state. Following my successful summit of Mount Rainier, I was feeling like a pro and set out to complete hiking all of Colorado's fourteeners. I thought I knew a lot, but I did not know at least one very important thing. I did not know what I did not know.

OUTDOOR SAFETY is a difficult concept to define. Safety is commonly understood to mean protection from harm, danger, or injury. As the Mount Lindsey story demonstrated, it is impossible to foresee and protect yourself from all dangerous events.

Those who study outdoor safety know this. They perceive hiking safety incidents as occurring along a continuum, from minor blisters due to poor-fitting boots to fatal falls when crossing exposed and dangerous slopes. These experts prefer the term "risk" and have borrowed from the corporate world the concept of risk management. Recognizing that no situation can be made 100 percent safe, they seek to mitigate risk through controls and risk strategies. For-profit, corporate entities have been despairingly described as using risk-management practices to protect the organization from legal claims, at the expense of customers. While it is rational for all organizations to seek to avoid litigation, in practice, risk management in the nonprofit outdoor education world seems to have a more benign history, that of seeking to learn from mistakes and protect and support its students.

Regardless of legal implications, risk and a degree of danger lie at the heart of all backcountry pursuits. Risk is often considered a major factor that contributes to the growth, self-awareness, and strength one takes away from wilderness adventures. While physical death may occur from traveling in nature, spiritual death can occur from not doing so. Environmental advocate Edward Abbey has said, "Wilderness is not a luxury, but a necessity of the human spirit."

In his book, *The National Outdoor Leadership School's Wilderness Guide*, outdoor educator Mark Harvey said, "Only your most honest and best traits will help you when you go out and test yourself in the wilds: judgment, patience, strength, and—dare I say this—character. . . . Nature insists on character."

Steve Smith, wilderness-experience thought leader and risk-management consultant, has written the seminal book on organizational safety practices. At first glance, it has the unassuming title of *Beneficial Risks*. But these two words say it all. There is significant risk in the outdoors, but it is well worth it. The *Appalachian Mountain Club Guide to Outdoor Leadership* also shares this viewpoint: "Risk presents an avenue for growth. Not all risk is bad." In the German language, there is the phrase, *einfallsreicher erfolg* or "resourceful success." It conveys the intense satisfaction one adds to life by learning how to survive risk through drawing on training, valor, ingenuity, and improvisation.

LEARNING BACKCOUNTRY SAFETY

Epistemology is the study of knowledge, of how we know what we know. Humankind acquires new information through various sources. Classically, knowledge is derived through intuition, educated guesses, learning from authorities, subject literature, and scientific methods. Scientific empiricism—based upon library research, creating a hypothesis, testing the hypothesis through experimentation, and statistically analyzing the data—is the gold standard, the most robust provider of replicable facts concerning natural phenomena. Over numerous centuries, the scientific method has become the bedrock of hard sciences, such as medicine, physics, mathematics, and social sciences, including psychology, sociology, and communications.

Unfortunately, the study of outdoor safety has been the beneficiary of minimal scientific research. There are relatively few examples of robust scientific analysis available regarding the outdoors. Where relevant empirical, quality studies have been published, they have been reviewed and their lessons included in this handbook. Those interested in the sources can find them in the "Sources and Recommended Reading" section at the back of the book.

However, what hiking and backpacking do have in abundance is many years of backcountry practitioner experience. Major hiking clubs have existed for over 100 years. Instructors, trip leaders, wilderness guides, youth education teachers, and outdoor educators have years of practical, hands-on, real-world experience from which we can all benefit.

Outdoor safety experts have long recognized the inherent worth of experience. Recently, there have been efforts to empirically demonstrate this value. Search and rescue teams have found it a reinforcing exercise to list the years of experience team members have, when preparing for a rescue. University of Colorado Professor and SAR expert Laura McGladrey has also recognized the value of the knowledge possessed by group elders. She has developed a simple measurement, the wisdom quotient. To obtain it, one divides the number of rescue participants by the number of years' experience of each member. The higher the quotient, the more capable and competent the team. Outdoor experience is an invaluable safety commodity.

HIKING EDUCATION

Hiking safety science may be limited, but the experience of fellow hikers is not. At the trailhead and on the trail, it is useful to ask returning hikers about their trip and trail conditions. Almost universally, they are friendly and can provide helpful information on water availability, animal encounters, and so forth.

Sometimes you may run into an informal hiker or climber code that exists among backcountry travelers. They may see your party undertaking a potentially dangerous activity but will decline to point it out to you. The code these people follow goes something like this, "I respect that each person must hike their own hike. I will not impose my experience upon others." Usually, the code makes an exception for intervening when children or

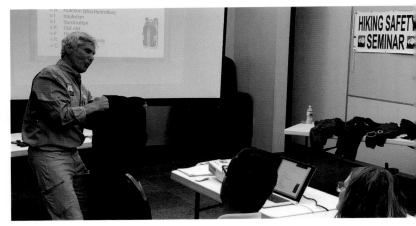

Hiking safety seminar

a life-threatening situation is obvious. Another major exception exists if you initiate a request for advice. Invariably, you will find that hikers, especially experienced ones, will go way out of their way to share knowledge, provide trail information, and help in an emergency. You only need to ask.

Hiking Clubs

A fun, user-friendly way to benefit from experience is to join a hiking club. These are often informal groups associated with a particular city or demographic, such as senior hikers or affinity groups. Participants report a wide range of quality in these clubs. They all share the advantage of having others to rely on for safety.

Typically, small hiking clubs do not employ paid staff and have safety practices that vary from trip leader to trip leader. Many small clubs have no specific requirements for trip leaders. These clubs usually have websites by which you can judge whether they match your interests and skills. Satisfied participants often find a competent trip leader and stick with that person's outings.

Although there are far fewer of them and they are more spread out across the United States, large hiking clubs typically have over a century of hiking experience, with substantial membership numbers, many volunteers, and paid staff.

As experience matters in hiking safety, these larger organizations tend to have more formal safety systems than smaller groups. Typically, their trip leaders are required to have current Wilderness First Aid and CPR certifications. In addition, potential leaders must attend leadership training. These organizations have formal safety protocols that leaders, instructors, and members must follow.

Even if you do not wish to join a hiking club, you can often find in-depth safety guidance on their websites. Frequently, they

MAJOR HIKING CLUBS	YEAR FOUNDED
Appalachian Mountain Club	1876
Mazamas Hiking Club (Portland)	1894
American Alpine Club	1902
The Mountaineers (Seattle)	1906
Colorado Mountain Club	1912
Wasatch Mountain Club (Utah)	1920
New Mexico Mountain Club	1952

Judge a Hiking Club by Safety

When selecting a hiking club, look for their commitment to safety. The best-run organizations will have dedicated safety and leadership committees, risk management committees, and a culture of fully reporting incidents and investigating all accidents and near misses. Instructors, leaders, and staff receive ongoing safety training and organizational support. Trip postings will provide risk information, appropriate gear to bring, and specifics concerning the rigor of each hike.

also have helpful safety publications and provide formal outdoor safety training, which is often open to nonmembers.

Outdoor Education Programs

There are increasing numbers of outdoor education programs. They are often associated with colleges or are stand-alone non-profits. Unlike hiking clubs, their curriculum leans toward using expanded field trips or expeditions as learning environments. College or professional credit is often available. Two well-regarded examples are the National Outdoor Leadership School (NOLS) and Outward Bound.

Guide-centered programs, on the other hand, focus more on mountaineering and climbing skills than hiking. However, these two sports blend, and one can learn many backcountry safety skills while in the presence of formally accredited mountain guides. Generally, guides will have either American Mountain Guide Association (AMGA) or International Federation of Mountain Guides (IFMGA) certification. RMI Expeditions, Exum Mountain Guides, and Colorado Mountain School are examples of well-respected organizations with guide-centered programs.

SAFETY STATISTICS

As a thoughtful hiker wishing to travel safely, you would be wise to be aware of the types of accidents that have befallen other outdoor travelers. Knowing what most likely can go wrong is a great tool to help you avoid making similar mistakes. This awareness is known as "risk literacy."

Outdoor recreation enterprises are expanding rapidly. Unfortunately, the compilation of safety data is scattered and has not kept pace with the growth of backcountry recreation. There are few consistent standards for recording incidents and their causes. Most outdoor travelers rarely report accidents unless seeking insurance coverage. For some, it is embarrassing to confide in others the errors they have made on the trail. Human nature leads us to want to be seen as competent and skilled in our pursuits.

The for-profit outdoor recreation industry has, in many cases, inherited operating practices from business and manufacturing entities. There are many incentives to not log accidents or scare away customers by sharing all past injuries and deaths. In legal matters, if it is recorded, accident documentation can be obtained through the discovery process and used against an organization in a lawsuit. Right or wrong, in our litigious society, organizations are mindful of their legal exposure. A keynote speaker at a recent outdoor risk-management conference pointed out that "the United States has 6 percent of the world's population and 51 percent of the world's attorneys."

Nevertheless, responsible outdoor organizations gather incident data and seek to learn from its implications. Hikers can benefit from knowing what, statistically, can befall them. Organizations that take safety seriously are the type you want to associate with in your outdoor pursuits. Nationally, leaders in safety data collection and analysis include the American Alpine Club, NOLS, the Appalachian Mountain Club, the Mountain Rescue Association, and the National Park Service.

Years of data review reveal certain patterns hikers will want to consider. Backcountry-user categories, such as skiers, climbers, kayakers, hunters, and mountain bikers, all report a significant number of injuries. However, no group comes close to hikers in the number of recorded wilderness incidents. In part, this is due to the very large number of individuals taking to the trails in recent years. While sports such as climbing and skiing are usually costly and require formal training, the entry point for hiking is very easily accessible, and almost anybody can head out for a day on the trail.

Hikers have a wide variety of experience and skills, but they share a typical set of injuries and maladies. By far the most common injuries that occur to hikers are strains, sprains, and broken bones. The single biggest cause of these trip-ending injuries are falls. Falls are also the primary reason for death among hikers. The uneven footing on trails is a leading cause, followed by scrambling on semi-technical terrain beyond one's ability. Traveling to exposed viewpoints, posing for selfies, and crossing snowfields are well-documented sources of wilderness falls.

In fact, 56 percent of all injuries are due to slips, trips, or falls. Terrain-related incidents are the single biggest cause of injury. In addition to dirt trails, "terrain" includes water hazards, such as flooding streams, semi-frozen lakes, and rapidly moving water. Hikers and backpackers have died fording streams and rivers, fishing near their campsite, packrafting, or falling into thawing streams and becoming trapped under ice sheets.

While mechanical injuries are the leading result of hiking accidents, illness is also a significant reason for backcountry emergencies. A surprising number of hikes are cut short due to intestinal issues. Abdominal pain, nausea, vomiting, and diarrhea together make up 33 percent of wilderness maladies. Causes are varied, but typical are reactions to uncommon levels of exercise, altitude, dramatic changes in hikers' diets, and untreated water. Backpackers suffer the most from abdominal issues, and here, the cause can almost always be traced back to camp hygiene. Well-meaning hikers share bags of gorp or nuts, offering them to others, who dig in with dirty hands. Camp dishes are often washed without boiling water and where stomach-disturbing soap residue often remains on pots and utensils. Backcountry handwashing can be minimal or nonexistent.

Backcountry toileting can add germs to hands, which, without washing and sanitizing, can get passed around at mealtimes.

The backcountry also reserves certain illnesses for its own that are much less common than in the front country. Dehydration and heat stress can both be killers, especially on hikes where you are working hard and water is in short supply. Conversely, hypothermia and cold-related issues due to low temperatures and precipitation are the leading causes of death among those lost in the backcountry. They account for about 6 percent of backcountry illness. Higher altitude brings on acute mountain sickness in 2.9 percent of hikers. Increasingly, mental health issues also surface among 6 percent of hikers, perhaps exacerbated by group dynamics, unaccustomed environments, or other causes of stress.

STAYING CURRENT

As previously mentioned, experience-based hiking clubs, guide services, and outdoor schools are a major source of safety knowledge. The best of these organizations maintain incident data and periodically evaluate it for potential lessons to be learned. They also benefit from sharing the experiences of similar organizations and safety practitioners. Toward this end, they will attend and participate in industry-wide educational events, such as the annual Wilderness Risk Management Conference (WRMC), cohosted by NOLS, Outward Bound, and the Student Conservation Association. This national conference, first convened in 1994, represents an outdoor-industry-wide event for responsible organizations to enhance safety standards. While aimed at organizations, unaffiliated individuals are also welcome to attend.

Learning never stops. Improved risk management is obtained over time and is a worthwhile goal for all outdoor practitioners. Keep safety skills strong through lifelong safety learning, steadily increasing your skill set through ongoing training and refresher courses. Competency can be derived from many sources. YouTube has many valuable resources and is easily accessible. There, you'll find the Colorado Mountain Club's Stephen Gladbach Memorial Moments safety videos particularly relevant, along with those created by the Colorado Fourteeners Initiative and NOLS. Magazines such as *Backpacker* are a useful read for all hikers and routinely include timely safety information. And, of course, so is this book and others like it. You will find many of them in the "Sources and Recommended Reading" section.

MAKE SAFETY A HABIT

Hiking can provide a lifetime of growth, personal enrichment, exercise, and fun. Safety is key to all of that. Establish a set of safety principles that fit well with the goals you have for wilderness hiking and exploration. Create a list of safety-related principles that you revisit before each trip you take. The list can be informal, will vary by type of trip, and will grow with your experience. With time, your list will become automatic. For example,

Big-Picture Safety Habits

Here are examples of safety habits that I have found useful over time. You can use these to inspire your own habits, ones that reflect your personal hiking goals and plans.

▶ Keep my Wilderness First Responder certification current. Periodically, check the NOLS Wilderness Medicine blog for protocol updates.

▶ Teach safety and first aid classes, which keeps me up to date. I also learn from student experiences and feedback.

▶ Yearly, practice ice axe self-arrest, so its use remains automatic in my muscle memory.

▶ Routinely read:
  - *Accidents in North American Climbing*, American Alpine Club
  - The "Accidents" report in *Appalachia Journal*, Appalachian Mountain Club
  - *Leadership Lines*, The Mountaineers blog
  - *Wilderness and Environmental Medicine*, Wilderness Medical Society

▶ Maintain and replenish the Ten Essentials I carry. Adjust seasonally. Take on all trips.

▶ Practice self-responsibility and be prepared to self-rescue on all trips.

▶ Always fill out a Leave a Trace Trip Plan and leave it with my wife or other responsible individual (see Appendix D).

▸ Know the fire danger status, weather forecast, and avalanche conditions before leaving on any backcountry trip.

▸ Check the websites of the National Park Service and US Forest Service before heading to any of those areas. Look under "notifications" and "warnings."

▸ Maintain current memberships to hiking and climbing clubs: American Alpine Club, Appalachian Mountain Club, Colorado Mountain Club, and the Mountaineers.

▸ Practice situational awareness on all trips. (For more on how to do this, see the following section.)

One instructor I know mentally reviews the Ten Essentials list (see page 119) before he drives to a trailhead. He does this every trip, and it helps him remember key gear. Another organizes all her gear in the same place—a basement closet—so it is easily refurbished and ready to go for each trip. This minimizes forgetting key items. Another instructor plans a minimum of one overnight trip every month so her skills remain sharp for longer adventures with more risk. These actions become habits and are easy, informal ways to foster a safety mentality.

SITUATIONAL AWARENESS

Developing a lifelong strategic approach to safety knowledge and practices is an important element of mastering the big picture of outdoor skills. Situational awareness is a narrower, field-level, tactical methodology that helps you sense problem situations and avoid them. It is the backcountry version of the "street smarts" that alert individuals practice in urban settings. We learn to walk city sidewalks with purpose and have our car keys in hand and ready to use when approaching our parked car at night—ideally, which we have left in a busy and well-lit garage. Eons of natural selection have provided us with a sixth sense to alert us to dangerous situations.

These same unconscious instincts can also be developed to keep us safe in wilderness settings. Situational awareness is basically increased alertness to our environment and what is going on around us. In many ways, situational awareness comes easier in the backcountry than in city settings. We are there, in part, to observe the beauty and wonders of nature around us. We are alert to and observe things not common to our workday lives. Changes in weather, the smell of woodsmoke, a moose and her calf—these all demand our attention. We can build on this natural awareness and fine-tune it with practice. The old saying on railroad crossing signs is a good start: "Stop, Look, and Listen."

Stop occasionally on your hike. What do you sense? Are there sudden gusts of wind (signifying an approaching front)? Turn around 360 degrees. Can you see and remember the landmarks you have passed? Are there other hikers around and approaching your location? A stop is a good time to look internally as well. Are you feeling tired, sore, light-headed, or energized?

Look around frequently as you progress. Turn your head to expand your range of vision. Do you sense movement? It is the most common way to detect animals otherwise well camouflaged in their environment.

Listen. Avoid earbuds, which can cover the sound of prairie rattlers or the huffing of brown bears. Do you hear voices of others in the area, an approaching mountain bike or ATV?

Situational awareness is a very wise skill to be practiced by both solo hikers and those in groups. Wilderness rescuers have long been trained in its benefits. In fact, called "scene size-up," it is taught as the very first action that rescuers and Wilderness First Aid practitioners should take when approaching the scene of a backcountry incident.

Before aiding a potential patient, all SAR personnel are taught to stop, closely observe the environment, identify potential risks confronting caregivers, and take proactive steps to minimize creating further victims—situational awareness at its best.

CHAIN OF ERRORS

Risk managers studying accident records have identified a phenomenon that appears again and again in incident analysis. Experienced rescue personnel recognize it, and it shows up repeatedly in safety literature. It is a variously called the "chain of errors," "the domino effect," "the cascade of bad events," or

Breaking a Chain of Errors

Safe hikers learn to tune in to an inner sense that things
are starting to go wrong. Certain occurrences trigger subtle
warnings, easily missed if you are not paying attention.
Individually, any one of the events listed here is not enough
to call it a day. But when you experience three or more,
it is wise to back off your hike and save your adventure for
another time. Some examples include:

▸ You brought one quart of water but meant to bring two.

▸ The quarrel you had with your spouse last night is preying
  on your mind. Your focus is not on the trail.

▸ It is a clear day, and you got an early start. You're several
  miles up the trail when the morning sun pops over a ridge,
  and you realize you left your sunglasses at home.

▸ The mosquitoes are out in force. You do not have any bug
  repellant.

▸ Your smartwatch, cell phone, or personal locator beacon
  indicate low battery power.

▸ Showers occur, and your rain gear "wets out," not repelling
  water and soaking through to your inner layers.

▸ The trail requires you to cross a raging stream on a
  snowbridge or slippery fallen tree. You must recross the
  same stream upon return, when snowmelt will make it
  faster and deeper.

▸ The trail is vacant of other hikers. When you do spot a person, they act strangely and dodge off the trail when spotting you.

▸ You can't remember if you locked your car and rolled up the windows.

▸ You're following "Leave No Trace" clothing guidelines by wearing dull green and gray clothing so you make less of a visual impact in the wilderness. You encounter dayglow-clad hunters and remember it is hunting season.

▸ You startle a large mammal that runs off into the brush. Five minutes later, you realize it has returned and is following you.

▸ You brought your tent for your overnight trip, but you forgot your tent poles.

"the ripple effect." Veteran mountain rescuer Mark Scott-Nash describes it as a "chain of seemingly unrelated incidents whose warning signs are not heeded." Sandy Stott, accidents editor at the *Appalachia Journal*, describes it as "bit by bit, that is how a hurt happens," and "the little increments which get us to a time and place where a whole slope lets go, or a cloud descends, when everything changes instantly."

The warning signs can be "outer" or "inner" signs. Examples of "outer" signs are visual evidence of recent avalanche activity or an overwhelming verbal disagreement among team members.

Examples of "inner" signs are your unease about conditions on the climbing route or the dynamics of the group, neither of which you can precisely put into words. Olympic champion gymnast Simone Biles courageously heeded inner warning signs when she withdrew from international competition in Beijing. Widely expected to win gold medals in her events, she said that she knew she should not attempt dangerous feats if her mental senses were exhibiting warnings. Skier Marc Peruzzi says, "If you aren't feeling it . . . , which is to say if your head isn't in the right place, it is best to back off."

BALANCING THE SCALES

A meaningful way to live life is to always strive to improve. Outdoor recreation skills contain a dilemma for which we need to be prepared: advancement in hiking, skiing, climbing, or kayaking all lead to additional risk. A 5-mile hike can prompt you to try a 10-mile hike, for example. A successful Class 3 climb motivates you to try a Class 4. The additional risk occurs as we progress in our proficiency, achieving the next step and anticipating what lies beyond, living on the edge of our skill boundary. This can be highly enriching. However, as risk increases, we need to also increase our training and equipment sophistication. Think of balanced scales as you add hiking challenges. Match them with increased knowledge and enhanced equipment.

THE REST OF THE STORY . . .

Somehow, I self-rescued from Mount Lindsey's flooding gullies. It required sliding, barely in control, down gullies of flowing mud and water. Then several hours of bushwhacking through head-tall, steel-wool-thick willows. I learned my lesson—which was that I had a lot more lessons to learn. I put my ego and back-country trips on hold and joined the Colorado Mountain Club. I signed up for hikes and worked my way up from an "A"-level (easy) hiker to "D"-level trip leader. I took every class offered and gained terrific partners with which to hike and climb safely across the West and around the world. And I did return to Mount Lindsey. This time the mountain gods conceded I had learned my lesson and let me summit.

2

Clothing

In March, my wife and I moved to Colorado from Ohio. Living in the Mountain West was our dream, and we wasted no time getting into the mountains—skiing, hiking, and climbing our first fourteener. In the last week of July, Colorado celebrated its centennial, turning 100 years old. So, it seemed like the perfect weekend to climb Mount Elbert, Colorado's highest peak.

We made a backpacking trip out of it, camping at tree line and climbing on July 31. Returning from the summit, we settled into our tent Saturday night as huge clouds built above us. The skies opened up, and rain fell for hours in a relentless deluge. Lightning landed all around our high mountain campsite. Concerned it would find our tent, we gathered all metal objects—our external-frame backpacks, metal pot, and stove. I put on a flimsy poncho and ran through the rain to dump them all 100 yards away. When I made it, sliding and stumbling, back to our tent, every item of clothing I was wearing was soaking wet.

IN THE BACKCOUNTRY, clothes can save your life. During an unexpected storm or unplanned overnight, they can make the difference between making it back to the trailhead or not. A classic piece of hiker's advice is that "there is no bad weather, only inappropriate clothes." Invest in learning some time-tested suggestions for appropriate clothing and you will add significantly to your wilderness safety and comfort.

Hopefully, on a hike, we leave a lot of things behind, things like our day-to-day routines, our pressing cares, and a sometimes-unhealthy inward focus. We also leave behind our air-conditioned cars and office buildings and our climate-controlled homes.

On the trail, our physiology takes over. The body's internal furnace burns calories to provide energy to keep us moving and warm. Your body strives to maintain a core temperature close to 98.6°F. Your systems work through a process called homeostasis to protect the vital organs from dramatic swings in temperature. A hiker's systems can only survive a very limited range of temperatures. Too hot and the result can be heat exhaustion or deadly heat stroke. Too cool and hypothermia results. Lower the body temperature to 82°F and death is certain.

As your body starts to heat up on the trail, the automatic homeostatic mechanisms trigger perspiration. Blood vessels in

Wet Clothes Can Be Dangerous

Wet clothes of any kind are a potential safety problem in the backcountry. They wick away precious warmth and can bring on cold-related injuries, such as frostbite or chilblains. Besides rain, one source of wetness that can sneak up on you and leave clothes wet before you know it is perspiration. Perspiration occurs as soon as you begin up the trail, especially if it is particularly hilly or you are carrying a heavy load. Experienced hikers head this off by starting out uncomfortably cool at the trailhead. After fifteen minutes or so, you should feel just right. Or, try starting off in a comfortable amount of clothing and stopping ten to fifteen minutes into your hike, as soon as you start to warm up, to remove a layer.

your skin enlarge as blood is increasingly pumped from a warming body core to the skin surfaces of your arms and hands, legs, and feet. There, it is cooled by the evaporation of sweat and conduction into the atmosphere.

The opposite occurs when the body's core begins to cool. Take too long of a break on your hike and the veins in your extremities start to constrict. Blood circulation is restricted to protect your body's core. If this process is allowed to proceed, your toes and fingers become cold, pale, and numb.

LAYERING

Layering is a simple, well-accepted technique for successfully dressing for a hike when changes in weather are expected. Except in hot conditions, you should carry three separate layers of clothes and add or subtract a layer as weather conditions and core body temperatures dictate. The three layers are a base layer, a middle layer, and an outer layer.

Base Layer

This is the bottom layer, closest to your skin. It should fit tightly to your skin so its most important function can take place: that is, wicking moisture away from the skin. It is the high-tech, syn-

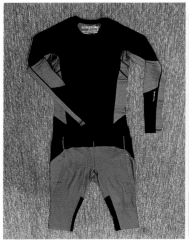

Base layers

thetic version of what earlier generations called long underwear. It can be found in light, medium, and heavy weights. You will also encounter expedition weight, which is used for high-attitude, extreme, multiday trips.

Bottoms should have elastic cuffs to keep out drafts and to fit under socks. Upper base layers usually come with round collars, but a quarter-zip collar is a great choice to help regulate body heat. It is your comfort choice to wear or not wear your regular underwear (boxers, briefs, bras) underneath this layer. Some individuals like the extra support they provide. If that is your selection, make sure these items are also made of wicking material, not moisture-holding cotton.

Base Layer Fabrics

Cotton and its progeny, denim, should be avoided. They easily soak up water, dry slowly, and remove body heat through evaporative cooling. While comfortable and useful in desert hiking, where their moisture-absorptive properties help keep you cool, cotton clothes fail almost all safety tests.

Polyester, with its water-repelling properties, is on the opposite end of the scale from cotton. It makes great long underwear, the surface layer of which is often treated to rapidly wick water, while the inner core repels moisture. Few garments dry faster than those made of polyester.

Polypropylene is popular for outdoor base layers. It readily repels water and allows garments to dry quickly. Its problems include retaining body odor and a low melting point, which makes it dangerous around campfires and backpacking stoves. Look for garments that have been chemically treated to combat these negative properties.

Silk was once a high-end choice for base-layer garments. It has a warm, luxurious feel that some hikers value, but it is expensive, its wicking properties are modest, and it is not odor resistant.

Lambswool is warm and retains some heat when wet, but it smells strongly, dries slowly, and can irritate sensitive skin. On the other hand, merino wool is rapidly becoming the first choice in moisture-wicking outdoor clothing. It dries fairly quickly, is very comfortable, and is very warm. It is ideal for next-to-skin layers and does not retain odors. A downside is that it can be costly.

Middle Layer

This layer is your warmth layer. Its purpose is to trap and hold heat radiating from your body. A wide range of materials are available. These include down, merino wool, and fleece. The key is having a material that traps air between its fibers. Air is an excellent insulator. The materials do not provide the insulation, rather it is the air pockets they enclose that retain your body warmth. Research has shown that the thermal insulation of clothing is proportional to the thickness of the dead air enclosed.

Hiking pants are the typical choice to wear over a base layer. In moderate weather, they can be worn without the base layer. They should be made of synthetic, quick-drying materials and often have a wide variety of zip pockets, cargo pockets, an elastic waist band, and built-in belt system. A popular choice is pants

Mid-layers

with zip-off legs that can serve the dual purpose of becoming hiking shorts. Tight, synthetic leggings are an alternative gaining in popularity for all sexes. They are comfortable and warm. However, they have snagging issues, and thicker versions hold moisture.

Mid-Layer Fabrics

Polyester fleece quarter-zip sweaters, jackets, or vests are an excellent first choice. Fleece comes in various thicknesses and weights and is warm, and few fabrics dry as quickly. It breathes well and is best paired with a windproof shell on windy days.

On cooler days, adding a puffy, insulated jacket is a wise choice. Choose one that can compress to a small size and take up little room in your daypack. Down is one of the warmest materials you can wear. It is derived from the under-plumage of ducks and geese and provides the greatest thickness per unit weight of any natural insulation. Historically, its major flaw is that it becomes useless when wet. Today, treated down that resists moisture is available. Manufacturers also combine down fill with synthetic fill for a material with a wide range of insulation in damp conditions. There are also 100-percent synthetic puffies. These are a good choice for activities near water and in wet climates. They are less expensive than down but are a little heavier to carry.

Outer Layer

This layer covers and protects your inner layers. Its key purpose is to keep heat-robbing wind and moisture out. Top-of-the-line shells are made of high-tech material that sheds rain but allows internal perspiration to escape. This can also be facilitated by a jacket that has numerous venting options, such as zippered armpit vents. Outer-layer rain pants cover your lower inner layers. These should fit loosely enough so you're able to easily use them to cover your mid-layer pants. Optional side zippers are highly desirable, so you can quickly don them without removing your boots, which is helpful when storms approach.

Outer-Layer Fabrics

Staying dry in the outdoors is a critical comfort and safety imperative. Your outer layers should be waterproof and, ide-

Outer layers

ally, breathable. Outer-layer shells come in several varieties. The most versatile is a waterproof-breathable "hard shell." This jacket prepares you for most bad weather and yet is lightweight and easily carried in your pack until you need it. These shells are usually nylon and coated with waterproofing or made of a laminated specialty fabric, such as Gore-Tex. Summit climbers need heavier, multilayer versions. Hikers can do well with lighter, single-layer versions. "Soft shell" jackets and pants are made of breathable, water-resistant material. They breathe well, are comfortable, add warmth, and are flexible, so movement is unrestricted. They resist light moisture but are not waterproof. They are useful in snowy conditions.

OTHER HIKING CLOTHES

It isn't always about layers. Other, accompanying pieces of cloth-ing can be worth their weight in gold on outdoor outings. Let's look at a few.

Hats

In the Mountain West, we are often at high altitudes with intense ultraviolet radiation and gusty winds. A wide-brimmed hat with a chin strap is a good choice. Buy one with breathable mesh in its crown. Treat it with a water-repellant spray and it will serve as a rain hat in light rain. If you expect heavy rain, retreat into the hood on your shell jacket. In these cases, hikers often find a baseball cap adds structure under the hood to help keep rain off the face. For safety and survival purposes, a wool or fleece "beanie" or watch cap should reside in your backpack year-round. In cold weather, it becomes your main headwear.

Gloves

Except in the hottest desert daytimes, you will be glad to have some kind of gloves with you year-round. An early European hiking guide I read said that you could always tell the foremost mountaineers because they never let their gloves get wet. This advice and my often-wet gloves perhaps confirm I am not among the ranks of elite mountaineers! Nevertheless, I agree that it makes good sense to do all that we can to avoid the annoying and possibly dangerous situation of wet gloves.

When buying gloves, seek those that have gauntlets or sleeves that keep snow and rain out of their openings. Treat them with a waterproofing product, and if snow or rain is expected, carry a spare pair. If the gloves do not have clips to pair them together, create your own by adding a small loop made of climbers' webbing and clip them together with a mini carabiner. Develop a rigorous habit of always clipping your gloves together when not in use. There are few backcountry happenings more annoying than losing a single glove.

Shoes and Boots

Your footwear is your foundation and connection to the terrain and helps ensure safe travel. The right shoes or boots can also help protect you from stubbing toes, breaking toenails, spraining ankles, and getting blisters.

Early hiking boots were thick soled, made of heavy leather, and often just about indestructible. They offered excellent safety from sharp trail dangers, protected weak ankles, and took months to break in. If they became wet, they took days to dry. Today, there is a staggering number of boots to choose from, and they are all much lighter than their predecessors.

While things have improved, there are still plenty of ways for footwear to trip you up. A comfortable, well-fitting boot is a safe boot. Spend plenty of time getting the best fit possible. Buy at long-established stores, with professional staff who can provide quality advice. The best stores have opportunities to return used, ill-fitting boots.

When you go to buy new footwear, take your preferred socks and liners to wear. Your feet expand during the day. Try for afternoon fittings, which will better match your hike-swollen feet.

The general rule is to wear heavier boots when carrying heavy pack loads and lighter boots or hiking shoes when carrying lighter gear. Trail-running shoes have become well accepted by hikers. Their low tops can be prone to collecting debris, stickers, and small rocks. They are popular with long-distance hikers who often solve the low-top problem by wearing gaiters. These are external, nylon sleeves that cover shoe tops and pants bottoms. In addition to keeping debris out, gaiters go a long way in helping feet stay dry and warm. Hikers are prone to ankle injuries. Stiffer, higher boots are thought to be safer for those with weak ankles.

Boots and hiking shoes are created on lasts, which are foot-sized model feet used by manufacturers. Over time, you will learn which brand's lasts work best for your individual feet. Lasts come in men's and women's models, but don't be afraid to try footwear from a different gender than your own. Many women, for example, say that they often have better luck with boots designed for men.

Be sure to check out the bottoms of your chosen footwear, as this is considered a safety feature. If you tend to hike where there are lots of boulders, slabs, and rocks, flat, sticky rubber soles and edges add dramatic stability. The same footwear can be slippery and dangerous on loose gravel trails. Sloping lugs or squarish rubber lugs are best for all-around trail safety. They grip well and limit sliding.

Boots and shoes often come with much longer laces than necessary. If you tie them as you would regular shoes, dangerous tails result, untying the knot or tripping you as you walk. Manufacturers supply the extra-long laces so you can tie a double knot ("surgeons knot") in several places as you lace up. Finish with a double-tied bow knot. Expect to retie your footwear as it settles in several miles along the trail. When first starting out, you will likely need to tighten your laces. After a long day of hiking, looser laces relieve swollen feet.

Extra shoes are rarely needed on a day hike. On backpacking trips, a lightweight sandal or camp shoe is a welcome luxury after a long day of hiking. Buy a pair that can provide double use as a water-crossing shoe or for walking if you have a boot loss or failure. From a safety standpoint, if you take sandals, always buy the kind that have a toe cover.

Socks

Socks are steadily increasing in variety and quality. A second pair is usually not needed for a day hike, but they are a lightweight safety backup that can be used for mittens, fire starters, bandages for hands and other body parts, or dressings. Merino wool socks are a great choice for hiking. Besides their comfort, they also have a reputation for minimizing blisters.

THE REST OF THE STORY . . .

The epic storm that hit our alpine campsite that night was widespread. One hundred miles to the north, it stalled for hours over the Big Thompson Canyon, creating massive flash floods. In what was cited as a thousand-year flood, 144 people died.

On Mount Elbert, we rose to clearing skies. All the clothes I had were soaking wet. We hiked out to the trailhead on badly washed-out trails. Other hikers we passed stared long and hard, as I wore the only dry item of covering I had left to wear, which was my nylon poncho.

3

Water Hazards

DON'T LET THIS HAPPEN TO YOU

Crystal Peak is considered a Centennial Peak, one of Colorado's 100 highest summits. When combined with a hike of nearby Father Dyer Peak, a popular trip was created, which I would lead the coming weekend. Although I had climbed the two peaks a few times in years past, I was out a week early, "safety scouting" the route to check for any anticipated surprises that might occur during our June trip. Regrettably, I found one.

Winter had been late in letting go, and a large, icy snowfield stretched across the standard ascent route. A slip on this section would send a hiker sliding 200 feet downhill, into a boulder field. I crossed the field carefully and, from the summit of Crystal, looked for a safer route to use the following weekend. I spotted a promising gentle slope to the south and headed for it. As I got closer, I discovered a downward-slanting meadow along

37

the route, which contained a 60-foot-wide gully filled with ice and snow. Later in the summer, this gully would host a mountain stream. The snow in the gully was large broken blocks but seemed very solid.

I started to cross and was partway when the ice began to slide downhill. I stopped, and the sliding stopped. I started again, and the sliding restarted. Again, I stopped, and again, the sliding ended. From below the ice, I could now hear rushing water. I knew enough about snow travel to know I was trapped on a wet avalanche chute.

WATER, IN ITS MANY FORMS, must be respected. Rivers, snowfields, glaciers, and frozen lakes cause more hiking deaths than wild animals, lightning, and forest fires combined. Factor water hazards into your trip planning, especially in the most dangerous winter and spring months. Carry proper water-safety gear, practice water-rescue techniques, and plan routes to avoid water dangers when possible.

WATER CROSSINGS

River and stream crossings are the most common water hazards hikers are likely to encounter. Maps may show bridges, but these backcountry spans can be damaged by winter storms and spring runoff. Trail-maintenance crews are lacking on public lands in much of the American West. It is considered above average for a trail to be surveyed once a year. A needed bridge replacement may take several years to be budgeted and completed.

When you arrive at a bridgeless river crossing above ankle depth, take time to scout the crossing. Is your trail clearly observable on the opposite bank? How fast is the water moving? Judge this by throwing a stick into the current and walking along the riverbank as it floats downstream. If the stick moves faster than you can walk, the river is too fast to cross.

Water depth can be gauged by dropping rocks in the river. A strong "kerplop" sound means it is likely above your knees and too deep to cross there. If the rock is pulled downstream or you hear it rolling on the bottom, a powerful current is present.

Err on the side of caution. River bottoms are slippery, and mountain streams can be bone-chillingly cold. If you have doubts, take the time to move up- and downriver, seeking a safer crossing. Better conditions often exist where the river is wide and braided. Where a stream narrows, it will be deeper and faster. Where it is wider, it will be shallower. Avoid river bends.

If a river crossing looks possible, improve your odds by using trekking poles or a wooden staff. Place all your critical gear on the inside of your pack, in plastic bags or river-runner dry bags. Unhook your pack's waist belt and sternum strap so you can swim free of your pack if you fall. If you have partners, post one upstream to watch for any floating hazards that might come your way, such as tree limbs. If not involved in a group-crossing technique (discussed below), all other group members should spread out downstream to help pull you from the river, if necessary.

Cross by facing upstream and sidestepping across, moving slightly downstream. Take only one step at a time. Crossing facing downstream can result in the current trapping a foot under a rock, an often-impossible predicament from which to escape.

For the same reason, if you do fall in, float on your back and lead with your feet downstream, keeping your toes above water and the rocks below. Backstroke to escape the strongest current. Seek a calm eddy to exit the river.

River Tides?

SAGE ADVICE

On the evening of the third day of a six-day wilderness backpack, my wife and I arrived at a necessary river crossing in a mountain meadow. An old, rough bridge was in place but was 90 percent submerged under dramatically cascading whitewater. It was held in tenuous place by a metal cable on the upriver side. River water flooded both the entrance and exit. Crossing under these conditions was impossible.

We pitched our tent next to the bridge and worried through the night that we would have to return the way we had come.

We were up early the next morning. In the rising sun, we saw that our bridge was now completely above water. Both ends stood on solid ground!

Do mountain streams have tides? No, we learned, but they do rise dramatically during the day as sunshine melts snow and fall at night when temperatures are cooler.

River crossings are highly dangerous. Be prepared to retreat and retrace your route, if necessary.

Crossing in a Group

Improve your stream-fording chances by crossing with group techniques. Several individuals working together dramatically improves everyone's stability.

Dry Crossing Techniques. These techniques depend on available physical supports on which to across. Crossing by walking on logs or downed trees may be the most obvious. They should be tested for stability and slipperiness before you commit to stepping on them. A slip can be jarring and dangerous. A fall on the upstream side of a log could force a hiker into a dangerous "strainer" situation where you are trapped under water by protruding tree branches.

Some rivers may be crossed on exposed rocks. Be aware that rocks tend to get wet and slippery as more hikers cross. Consider having weaker team members cross second and be assisted by a strong member who has previously crossed.

Group Pole Technique. Here, a wood pole or two trekking poles, duct-taped into one, are held by three hikers. All hold the pole horizontally with two hands and cross facing upstream.

Conga Line Technique. In this method, three to five hikers line up front to back behind a strong lead hiker who creates a bit of

Top: Group pole technique **Left:** Conga line technique **Right:** Paired technique

a river eddy with their body. The lead hiker steadies themselves with a hiking pole or stick, and the other hikers hold the pack straps or waist belts of those in front of them. The group faces upstream and moves sideways across the river.

Paired Technique. Two hikers can cross a river using this method. The hikers face each other, one upstream and one downstream. The stronger person is upstream and takes the first step. The downstream person matches it and so on, across the river. This also works well with three individuals holding onto each other in a triangle.

River Clothes

Your pants will get wet crossing a moderate or deep river. In cool weather, this creates another problem for you. Change into shorts before crossing. Removing your pants also lets you move more easily through the water.

If you have river shoes, wear them. Carry your boots tied securely to your pack. If you don't have river shoes and the bottom is sandy or muddy, you can try just wearing socks. The safest method is to remove your socks, keep them dry, and cross in your boots. If you do this, remove the footbed insoles first and keep them dry as well. Dry your feet after crossing. Your dry socks and dry foot beds will help your boots dry more quickly.

Tyrolean Traverse. Crossing a river with a rope is an advanced technique, well beyond the scope of this book. It may be tempting to tie a perceived safety rope, knotted in front, to the waist of an individual wading or swimming across a river. A dangerous trap occurs if the crosser slips in the current. The rope can tighten and pull the individual facedown underwater. Don't attempt rope use until you have adequate water rescue training.

SNOWBRIDGES

Each year, collapsing snowbridges claim the lives of backcountry hikers. Snowbridges are structures of compacted fallen snow that cover glacier crevasses, ice cracks, and most commonly, streams and rivers. Their benign surface appearance can hide dangerous terrain. Unsuspecting travelers can fall through stable-appearing surface snow to incur an injury, drown, or freeze to death in hidden, rushing meltwater.

Snowbridge incidents occur most often in the spring and early summer months. A widely reported snowbridge fatality occurred to Kings Canyon National Park backcountry ranger Randy Morgenson, whose July 1996 disappearance launched years of mystery and searches. His remains were eventually discovered five years after he went missing. Ranger Morgenson's death was determined to be due to a collapsing snowbridge, associated injuries, and hypothermia.

Snowbridges are dangerous because it can be impossible to judge what is happening below a snowy surface. Often, streams erode snowbanks from below, until the surface can no longer hold the weight of a hiker. Hikers may be tricked by following the footprints of earlier trekkers who crossed the bridge when the snow could still support a traveler's weight.

Snowbridge Photo by Steve Billig

Stay observant. Look for sagging snow surfaces. Sometimes the sound of running water is also a giveaway. You can also study topographic maps whose blue lines indicate the location of year-round running streams. Use extra caution when traveling in these areas.

If you suspect a snowbridge exists, try probing with a trekking pole. Breaking through a surface crust to open space below is a danger sign and reason to immediately retreat. Never completely trust a snowbridge, even in deep winter. If your group must cross a snowbridge, do so one at a time and move out of the danger area before another person crosses.

THIN ICE

High-altitude lakes can remain ice covered well into summer. Avoid frozen lakes if you can. If your trip involves extensive ice travel, wear a life jacket and carry ice picks. Test the ice depth

Left: Dangerous gray ice **Right:** Snowslide danger

with an ice axe, timber axe, or stout pole. Ice less than four to six inches thick should not be trusted. New, clear ice is stronger than old ice. White or dirty-looking ice is weaker than clear ice. Ice with one crack is 40 percent weaker than ice with no cracks. Two cracks intersecting one another weakens the ice by 75 percent. At any time, even well-frozen lakes can have thin spots due to subsurface springs or shallow areas. A lake that has, for years, been reliably solid can, after a summer with sediment runoff due to isolated microbursts, develop shallow water weak spots.

If the worst happens and you do fall through thin ice, do what you can to control your immediate panic. Your body's response will be to gasp (hyperventilate), which causes you to suck in water if your head is below the surface. In and of itself, this is a potentially deadly reaction. Turn around to the direction you entered the water. You know the ice in that direction has held your weight. The strength of the ice in other directions is unknown. You will rapidly lose strength while you are in the water. Make strenuous attempts to get back on the ice as quickly as possible. Throw your arms onto the ice while kicking aggressively. If you have trekking poles, grasp them just above the baskets and use them as ice picks to help you gain traction on the ice surface. Other tools people have used include knives, tent stakes, and wet forearms pressed against the ice. Clothing (sleeves) can freeze to the ice after a few minutes and provide a grip. As you start to pull yourself out of the hole, move your legs high in the water so your body becomes parallel with the ice surface. Proceed to pull yourself out. When you are on the ice, stay on your stomach to keep your weight distributed. Crawl until you reach safe ice or the shore.

If you have a partner with you, they should avoid becoming a victim as well. They can help by extending a tree limb or rope. Once you are out of the water, they can assist you into dry clothes and by building a fire.

AVALANCHE

Avalanches have proven deadly to skiers, snowshoers, snowmobilers, and climbers. And although less common, they claim the lives of hikers each year. Colorado leads the Western US in avalanche deaths, followed by Alaska, Utah, Wyoming, and

Washington. While January is the deadliest month, avalanche deaths have occurred every month of the year.

Hikers should be alert to the basic parameters of avalanches. Snow avalanches are slides that rapidly move down slopes. They range in size and can be dry or wet. Dry avalanches are powdery and the kind usually seen in newscasts. Wet avalanches tend to occur in the spring and early summer. They do not billow, rather they flow like rivers.

Three key ingredients are required for an avalanche to occur: avalanche terrain, unstable snow, and a trigger. An avalanche will not happen without all three of these factors:

▸ **Avalanche terrain** is found on slopes steeper than 25 degrees, about the angle of a blue diamond-rated ski slope. Slides occur at lower angles, but they are very rare. Low-angle slopes can be triggered after being fed by higher, steeper slopes. Avalanches also tend to occur in steep gullies and near cliff faces. Today, many compasses contain a mechanical inclinometer, which allows you to measure slope angles, and electronic versions are available for smartphones.

▸ **Unstable snow** is snow that is loaded and ready to release. It is said to be "wanting" to slide downhill. Snow stability is influenced by many factors, including the age of the snow (newer snow is more prone to slide), weather, precipitation history, melting, and wind effects. Judging snowpack stability accurately requires formal training and field observations.

▸ **Triggers** of avalanches include fresh snow, mountain rains, and wind gusts. These triggers are considered natural occurrences. In remote areas, these slides may never be observed. Accidental avalanches are those typically triggered by humans. Victims can bring on an avalanche by traveling across unstable snowfields. Releases triggered by one traveler can cascade and engulf others in the vicinity. Avoid traveling directly below parties that are higher up the slope.

Know Your Closest Avalanche Center

All the previously mentioned warning signs and dozens of others are used by meteorological scientists to create formal avalanche forecasts. Forecast centers spread across the American West broadcast safety messaging of current and future avalanche conditions. (See Appendix E for a list of US avalanche centers.)

Their free notices can be found online and on smartphone apps, and include danger warnings based on the likelihood, size, and distribution of avalanches. They provide easy-to-understand, color-coded scales ranging from low to extreme danger levels (Their scale is known as the North American Avalanche Danger Scale.)

Avalanche Danger Signs

Hikers in snowy areas should scan slopes for signs of recent avalanche activity. Slides leave telltale signs of broken cornices, fracture lines, and debris fields of jumbled snow blocks. Broken trees and branches are obvious indications of avalanche activity. Listen for a "whumping" sound. This loud and distinct noise is the sound of settling snow, often triggered by your presence. Leave the area immediately. Expect avalanche activity after recent heavy snowfall or rainfall. Rapid temperature changes and strong winds also forecast snowpack instability.

Avalanche Classes

All hikers should understand avalanche dangers well enough to avoid slide-prone areas entirely. Those whose travels take them into exposed areas should have formal avalanche safety training. Fortunately, these classes are readily available. They are provided by avalanche education nonprofits, mountain clubs, outdoor retailers, and the Forest Service. Courses follow recreational and professional tracks. Recreational mountain hikers will find great benefit in awareness classes, also known as Avalanche Terrain Avoidance (ATA). These classes usually have classroom and field elements. They cover avalanche phenomenon, causes, and risks. They focus on teaching you to recognize avalanche terrain so it can be avoided.

If you want or need to travel in areas with avalanche potential, more advanced skills are necessary. These multiday classes are known as Level 1 Avalanche Courses. The American Institute

Crossing Snowfields and Avalanche Chutes

Forced to cross a snow couloir or possible snowfield avalanche chute? Here are some safety tips:

▸ Tighten your pack straps to help maintain balance.

▸ Zip zippers, and wear hat and gloves.

▸ Remove your hands from the straps of your hiking poles.

▸ Cross one group member at a time.

▸ Move from safe zone to safe zone ("islands of safety"). From safe locations, others should closely watch the next person crossing.

for Avalanche Research and Education (AIARE), a well-regarded organization, coordinates course content and offerings of associated training organizations.

FLASH FLOODS

In rural areas, where many of us like to hike and camp, flooding has long been the leading weather cause of fatalities. Floods kill more people than tornadoes, hurricanes, or lightning. Floods are most often caused by heavy rain or rapid snowmelt. Water

Flash flood danger is high in burned areas.

overflows onto land that is typically dry. Flooding usually lasts from several days to weeks.

Flash floods are a highly dangerous subcategory of floods. They happen quickly and wreak explosive havoc, often moving downstream with incredible speed. They are most often caused by lingering cells of heavy rainfall, falling rapidly in focused locations. The mountains, steep hills, and desert canyons we enjoy contribute to flash flooding. Rocky slopes and clay soils are unable to quickly absorb significant moisture. Hiking trails often travel through narrow canyons and alongside creeks and rivers. Elsewhere, they follow dry riverbeds and arroyos. Traditionally, these areas can become death traps when flash floods occur.

As the Western US experiences dramatically increasing wildfires, burned-over areas are producing more and more flash floods. These flash floods are particularly dangerous due to the heavy volume of fire debris they carry. Hikers need to be vigilant for flash floods. The rainfall that generates a flood can occur miles upstream from your location. In fact, it can be sunny and dry where you are when a wall of flood water arrives. You may have little or no warning. It is unlikely you can outrun a flash flood.

Climb the slopes from your location to a higher elevation. Be aware that rapidly rising water can reach heights of 30 feet or more. Take steps to protect yourself from flash floods by closely monitoring weather reports. The National Weather Service uses specific terminology in its alerts:

Flash Flood Watch or Flood Watch: Flash flooding or flooding is possible within a designated watch area. Be alert.

Flash Flood Warning or Flood Warning: Flash flooding or flooding has been reported or is imminent. Take necessary precautions at once! Get to high ground!

If you are hiking flood-prone areas, be extra alert. Look for water-channel areas that show evidence of past flooding, such as scoured areas devoid of vegetation or broken tree branches or tree trunks that have been forced into canyon walls above your head. If there is evidence of past flooding, know that it can happen again. Follow the National Weather Service flood mantra, "Turn around, don't drown."

THE REST OF THE STORY . . .

I was trapped in the middle of a wet avalanche chute, which seemed to be playing with me. I was safe as long as I didn't move. So, I didn't move. I took my time, ate a snack, and drank some water. It was a cold place to be, so I added clothing layers.

I knew I would have to move eventually. I developed a plan that was pretty basic.

In my mind, I carefully visualized each step I would take to reach the other side of the gully. I said my good-byes, took a deep breath, and went for it. The avalanche immediately came to life and started moving amazingly fast downhill. I kept leaping as quickly as I could. One final jump and I gained the opposite bank of the meadow. The avalanche had carried me downhill about 150 feet. Now, it did not stop but crashed and slid down the remainder of the gully and cascaded over a cliff edge. Scratch the alternate route!

4

Weather

It was spring break, a great time to get outdoors and visit the desert before it became too hot to hike. We drove all day and arrived at Arches National Park around 2:00 p.m. on a sunny, 60°F afternoon. We knew Arches was a crowded park that limited backpacking, but we had devised a clever plan. We would park our car at the Delicate Arch Trailhead (no longer allowed) and hike for 2 miles, leave the trail, cross the park border, and camp on unrestricted Bureau of Land Management (BLM) land.

The trail took us into an amazing world of sandstone canyons and arches. We hiked along the tops of rock fins, following rock cairn trail markers. There was a lot to see, but what we missed was a rapidly darkening western sky. Our pleasant afternoon was brought abruptly to a halt as very high winds hit like a freight train. The winds carried sand, dust, dirt, rain, snow, and probably a cactus or two. As the sun disappeared and the skies darkened, we added clothing layers. We draped rain ponchos over our packs and ourselves. In the high winds, these proved useless as they billowed like sails. We hunched behind boulders, soaking wet and cold.

OUR HOMES ARE HAVENS OF COMFORT. A flip of a thermostat switch adds warmth or cool air as desired. Strong sunlight can be shut out with curtains, and rain is stopped by a shingled roof. We can judge the wind by looking out the window at swaying trees or plants, but safe inside, we don't feel it.

Traveling in nature, however, we are literally immersed in the weather. Activities such as hiking, backpacking, and climbing take us out of safe homes and often miles from the sanctuary of automobiles. Directly experiencing changing weather can be exhilarating if we are aware of its vagaries and have consulted predictions. When we plan ahead, weather can be one of the great joys of outdoor life. On the days leading up to your trip and throughout your journey, you should monitor weather patterns.

EVALUATING WEATHER

Formal weather forecasts are remembered when they clearly get things wrong. However, most of the time they come pretty close to predicting the weather we can expect. They are most accurate closest to the time of your departure. Several days before a back-country trip, it is wise to start noticing weather forecasts and patterns for the area of your planned hike. Look at the projected daytime temperatures and precipitation forecast. Check to see if they are normal for the time of year or are changing. Even if you are only planning a day trip, it is important to check the coming nighttime temperatures and prepare for surviving overnight, in case of an accident.

Generic local TV and radio forecasts are useful for the city and suburban areas where most of us live. Their greatest strengths for hikers are the regional maps that show approaching weather fronts and pressure zones. Otherwise, they are not

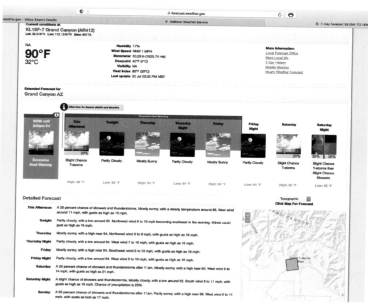

Weather.gov Grand Canyon weather forecast

always helpful for the locations where we like to hike and back-pack. For example, if you plan to head to mountains or foothills, remember temperatures drop by about 4°F for each 1,000 feet of altitude you gain. River basins and riparian zones can be mark-edly cooler than nearby slopes. Impassable snowfields continue to bury mountainside trails into summer and long after snow monitoring (SNOTEL) stations report that all is clear.

National Weather Service

The National Weather Service (NWS) of the National Oceanic and Atmospheric Administration provides hikers with almost NASA-space-launch levels of scientific weather data. Once you have selected a hiking location, their truly amazing website, weather.gov (not to be confused with weather.com!), can tell you what weather occurred there yesterday, what will happened today, and what to expect next week. It can tell you if a river crossing will be too deep to cross next month, if the snow on the ground is heavy or fluffy, how windy your trip will be, and if there is signifi-cant wildfire potential along your selected trail. Time spent on the website prior to your trip will yield huge safety rewards.

Start by visiting the NWS home page. On the United States map, all counties in the country are displayed. Those that are col-ored are experiencing some sort of serious weather alert. Scroll down for the key to what the colors represent, for example high wind warnings, blizzard warning, flood advisory, and so forth.

Obtain a local forecast for your hiking location by entering its zip code, the nearest town, or the name of a major geological landmark, such a pass, mountain peak, or lake. It will provide you with today's and tonight's forecast. Click on the "Get Detailed Info" line. You now have a detailed six-day forecast for your general hiking area. Forecasts are updated about every four hours, so if you are going on a multiday backpack, print it out (in color) the morning of your trip and take it with you.

Also on this page, you will see a topographical map with a green 2.5-kilometer block at the center. That square represents the precise location for which the forecast has been tailored. You can modify it for satellite or street views. The location box conforms to the general landmark location you provided. You can now zoom out on the map to find the precise trail you have selected. Drag the pointed-finger curser to this spot and click. The software will now provide a forecast for the exact trailhead you have selected.

As an example of how this works, consider the town of Estes Park, Colorado, the gateway to Rocky Mountain National Park. Most newspaper, cell phones, and TV weather maps can give you a good forecast for Estes Park. The NWS weather website will do this as well. But you are going to enter the park and hike Bear Lake, 5 miles to the west and thousands of feet higher than Estes Park. When you drag the pointer from Estes Park to the Bear Lake Trailhead, you may find it is very windy and snowing heavily, very different weather from Estes Park. Something you definitely want to know and prepare for!

You can obtain further customized weather reports by using the website's "User-Defined Area Forecast" feature. Imagine you have planned a weeklong, wide-ranging backpack into Montana's Glacier National Park. You want information for the entire area you plan to cover. On the weather.gov homepage, again find the United States map. Click on the general area of Glacier National Park. This will take you to the closest of 122 NWS forecast offices in the US. Each state has two to four such regional offices. You are now at the NWS forecast office based in Missoula, Montana. On the subject line, click on "forecasts." In the dropdown box that appears, you will see the option of "User-Defined Area." From here, you can create an individualized forecast for the entire area you plan to hike. You encircle your target area with draggable markers, allowing you to obtain a one-of-a-kind, customized forecast for your entire trip.

Other Weather Services

There exists a wide range of commercial weather services. Most of them base their analysis on National Weather Service data, at least in part. Hikers and climbers who closely follow weather forecasting often find a service they believe works well for their personal needs. Many of these have free basic services and charge for advanced options. There is a certain amount of flux among these providers, as they add new features, drop little-used options, and frequently merge with other services.

A useful practice is to explore some of these providers and compare their ease of use and accuracy with the NWS reports. Choices most often recommended by outdoor enthusiasts include:

▸ **pivitolweather.com.** Recommended by meteorologists and weather geeks who hike and climb. Users can access and compare numerous weather models for in-depth analysis.

▸ **mountain-forecast.com.** A highly comprehensive service focused on worldwide mountain weather.

▸ **opensummit.com and opensnow.com.** Hourly forecasts tied to actual mountain peak locations.

▸ **weatherunderground.com.** A popular service that compliments NOAA data with a network of 250,000+ personal weather stations.

▸ **weatherbug.com.** Is often cited as the choice of climbers, who value its lightning maps.

▸ **accuweather.com.** A popular site with a reputation for accuracy and ease of use.

ASSESSING WEATHER ON THE TRAIL

Once you are on the trail and off the grid, you leave high-tech weather reporting behind. You must now rely on your own knowledge and senses as you interact with the natural world. This can be one of the true joys of the outdoors.

Most backcountry hikes start in the morning. If the night before was clear, you can expect a cool or cold start, depending on the season. Most early mornings are calm. If conditions are windy from the start, expect weather to deteriorate during the day. Fog in the early morning that slowly burns away promises fair weather.

Top: Cumulous clouds **Bottom:** Stratus clouds

As your hiking day progresses, pay attention to the sky. Is there cloud cover that begins to lift? The weather will improve. Does the sky darken? Expect rain or snow.

Cloud Formations

Observing cloud formations is one of the best ways to predict approaching weather patterns.

The weather will worsen if you see:

▸ clouds start to stack in enormous columns
▸ clouds thicken and descend closer to the earth
▸ clouds become particularly dark to the west.

The weather will improve if you see:

▸ clouds ascend higher in the sky
▸ clouds separate and diminish in size
▸ blue patches increasingly appear between clouds.

Cloud Types

The type of clouds you observe can offer valuable clues to coming weather. Two major categories of clouds are common:

▸ **Cumulous clouds:** Puffy and not too high in altitude, they can indicate showers later in the day.
▸ **Stratus clouds:** Appear as sheets or layers. They are close to the earth, can appear as fog, and are associated with precipitation.

Left: Altocumulous clouds   **Middle:** Altostratus clouds   **Right:** Cumulonimbous clouds

Clouds are also classified based on their altitude. The prefix "alto" is added to indicate middle; "cirro" is added to indicate high. When the suffix "nimbo" is added, it denotes rain.

- **Altocumulus clouds:** Middle-height and puffy clouds that often predict thunder and rain showers.
- **Altostratus clouds:** Middle-height, layered clouds that indicate rain in forty-eight hours.
- **Cumulonimbus clouds:** Originate as low-level cumulus clouds and grow to giants that can rise to 37,000 feet. They form towering, blocky, anvil-shaped thunderheads and often quickly produce hail, lightning, snow, and high winds.

WEATHER FRONTS

Tracking weather fronts is a key way to predict the weather you can expect in the coming few days. Fronts occur when very large air masses of different temperatures and densities collide, creating a frontal boundary. These masses do not mix. One will dislodge another.

Warm fronts rise over cooler air, and cold fronts will push underneath warm air. Either action causes turbulence and air to be lifted. Depending on temperatures, if moisture is present in the upswell, it will turn to rain or snow. Warm fronts are massive, often extending over 800 miles. They move slowly, indicating their approach with high, wispy clouds that lower over one or two days to become stratus clouds. At night, their approach is forewarned by a halo around the moon. As they advance over cooler air ahead, precipitation often occurs. Because warm fronts move so slowly, rain can last for days.

Cold fronts occur when cold air arrives quickly and slides under warm air, pushing it higher and causing it to cool. Cold fronts are much smaller than warm fronts, generally closer to 100 miles wide, and they move more quickly. Their arrival often generates heavy precipitation and violent weather. Cold fronts are often marked on their leading edge by high winds and a narrow band of thunderheads. Known as a squall line, this phenomenon can topple trees, tip canoes, blow away tents, and knock over hikers crossing passes.

Barometric pressure is the pressure created by all the weight of the atmosphere upon any given point on the earth's surface.

Nature's Weather Forecast

Satellite-enabled weather forecasts and meta computers crunching data have earned their place in weather forecasting. But before they existed, nature provided her own clues. Here are some tips on recognizing nature's signs to predict weather.

Smells are heightened. The humid air that develops before a storm helps smells dispense. More water particles in the atmosphere help carry odors to your nose.

Birds fly high. Soaring birds indicate clear, calm weather. They stay close to the ground when the low air pressure of an approaching storm makes flying difficult.

Pinecones close. The humidity of storm conditions signals pinecones to close to protect their seeds. They reopen in dry air to help disperse those seeds.

Red sky in the morning. The old sailors' warning that red morning skies harbor approaching storms contains wisdom. The rising sun reflects off the eastern clouds, indicating moisture in the atmosphere and storms that are likely by day's end.

Animal behavior changes. Butterflies and bees retreat from fields of flowers before storms. Deer, elk, and mountain goats move from high ridges to wooded valleys. Cattle herds group together, as do horses, who turn their backs to the approaching weather. Grazing animals know when winter storms are coming, and they eat heavily as they expect snow to cover their feeding areas.

Frost or dew on vegetation. A clear night that leaves morning dew on plants signals the day will likely be pleasant.

Barometric pressure affects mood. Falling barometric pressure can bring on a heavy, lethargic feel, along with headaches. High energy derives from crisp and light brisk air associated with high air pressure and clearing weather.

Smoke signals. Smoke plumes raising straight up from a campfire indicate high pressure and nice weather. Smoke remaining near the ground signals low pressure, with rain likely.

Rainbows to the west. Rainbows are always beautiful. But if you see one in the west in the morning, expect rain.

It is, perhaps, the most important indicator of changes in weather. Moisture-laden air is lighter than dry air and associated with low-pressure systems. Expect a storm. Barometric pressure that is rising is usually associated with fair-weather systems and high air pressure. Hikers' watches often measure altitude and barometric pressure. Such watches can be a useful tool to alert you to changing weather.

HYPOTHERMIA ALERT

Weather that is cold, wet, and windy is unpleasant. It can also be deadly to hikers. Hypothermia, also known as exposure, is the number one weather-related cause of death in the mountains. Foul-weather travelers should educate themselves about this condition and learn to spot its signs and symptoms. Because it can be so dangerous to hikers, I am including the topic in this safety handbook, but this is not a Wilderness First Aid manual. All backcountry enthusiasts are encouraged to take a class that leads to certification in Wilderness First Aid, a category of emergency care designed for the unique circumstances encountered in remote locations.

Hypothermia is a life-threatening condition that occurs when the body's core temperature falls below 95°F (35°C). It can occur whenever one's heat loss exceeds heat gain. It can develop year-round and even indoors. Pay attention when anyone in your hiking group is wet, miserable, and cold.

Hypothermia can be forestalled by moving to a shelter, consuming high-calorie food and drinks, and engaging in warming exercises. These early signs are called *cold stress* and, if foul weather conditions continue, can lead to the classic stages of hypothermia.

A telltale sign that a person is progressing to hypothermia is vigorous, uncontrollable shivering. This is the body's involuntary effort to warm itself. Shivering can be accompanied by apathy, clumsiness, and the "umbles." These are behaviors that a person exhibits and include mumbling, grumbling, stumbling, fumbling,

Keep a Watch Out

In cold, windy, and wet conditions, keep an eye on your hiking partners' welfare. Occasionally ask the group how everybody is doing. Those who are fine will say so. Watch for those who do not reply, as they may be struggling. Another classic tell that someone is struggling with the cold is the hiker who tries to zip up their jacket but is unable to and gives up. If you see that, it's time to assess circumstances and seek shelter.

and tumbling. These responses indicate a deteriorating condition and an altered mental state.

The most dangerous form of hypothermia is described as severe. Here, a person stops shivering, they are unable to walk, and their skin appears blue. In worst cases, the person may appear dead, and it can be difficult to detect breathing and pulse (heartbeat).

Without Wilderness First Aid or medical training, you are very limited in the assistance you can render. But there are steps you can take that will help the stricken individual:

▸ Treat anyone suspected of hypothermia gently and be supportive.
▸ Assist the person to shelter and replace wet clothing.
▸ Place insulation beneath and around the person.

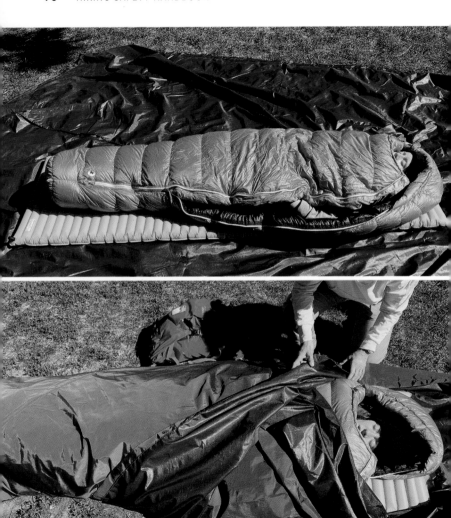

Top: Patient placed in hypothermia wrap **Bottom**: Patient wrapped as a burrito

▸ Determine if nearby hikers or campers have medical training and can assist.

▸ It is appropriate to activate search-and-rescue assistance for cases of hypothermia.

▸ While waiting for assistance, you can do no harm by creating what has been described as a "tried and true" backcountry warming tool, the hypothermia wrap. With the individual in dry clothes, place them in a sleeping bag on top of a foam sleeping pad. If available, place additional sleeping bags over and below the person. Wrap a waterproof ground sheet or tarp around the sleeping bags to keep them dry and protect them from the wind. This has also been described as a burrito wrap. Do not cover the person's face. You can provide heat sources in the form of hot water bottles. One goes in the person's hands and one at their feet. Be sure to test the water bottles against yourself to make sure they are not too hot. Insulate the water bottles with dry socks.

THE REST OF THE STORY . . .

After we had been hiding from the storm for thirty minutes, the squall moved off as fast as it had come. We emerged wet and shivering from our hiding spot to find the trail invisible under two inches of snow. It was an easy decision to call off our planned overnight. It was not easy, however, to make our way back to the trailhead. The rock fins we had easily crossed when dry were now ice-covered and slick. Only by locating rock cairns one by one could we find our way out. As we slowly progressed along the route, the sun setting in the west broke through storm clouds. It brilliantly illuminated an Arches National Park phenomenon known as the Fiery Furnace. Truly stunning! This greatly lifted our spirits. We made it to the trailhead just after dark and to a motel room an hour later. The tidy motel room quickly became a jumble of damp ponchos, clothes, and packs. And we had another memory and a hard lesson about weather to remember.

5

Lightning

My college roommate and his wife were on a Rocky Mountain road trip from the Midwest. After a week in Aspen to acclimatize, they wanted to meet, backpack, and climb their first fourteener. With its Class 2 routes and a 12-mile hike that could be tempered with an overnight backpack camp, Mount of the Holy Cross fit all their requirements. Plus, it was on my peak list, and I was eager to check it off.

We met at the trailhead during a classic Colorado afternoon monsoon thunderstorm. We sat out the rain in our cars, and when the storm cleared, we carried heavy packs over Half Moon Pass and camped near East Cross Creek. Despite the wet start, it was great to see good friends, and we stayed up late enjoying a campfire and catching up. We were slow to start the next morning, not hitting the trail until 10:00 a.m. But we made good time and were soon on the north ridge of Holy Cross. We passed out of the trees at 11,600 feet and entered the talus slopes on unmaintained trails. The stunning ridgeline views made up for the awkward footing. That is, until we realized that also in view was a rapidly darkening western sky. We were new to hiking lofty mountains but had heard the admonition, "Be off the summit and high ridges by eleven." It was 1:00 p.m., and we only had a mile to go. We had put a lot of effort into getting this close, and it felt defeating to back out now. After all, when would we get this chance again?

Two of our party opted to return to the campsite and wait out any rainstorm. My roommate, however, followed my questionable lead and agreed to push on. We lightened our packs into those of the descending team members, promising that we would quickly move to the summit, "tag it," and descend immediately. We found ourselves scrambling for the summit as the clouds closed in around us.

IN THE ROCKY MOUNTAIN WEST, June, July, and August host the busiest hiking season. Unfortunately, these months also parallel with prevalent thunderstorms and high numbers of injuries due to lightning. While overall deaths have decreased due to outdoor safety education efforts, lightning encounters have risen as more people pursue hiking, climbing, mountain biking, camping, fishing, and other wilderness activities. When incident statistics are weighted for population, Montana, Wyoming, Colorado, Utah, and New Mexico rank in the top ten states for lightning casualties.

THUNDERSTORMS

All thunder is the result of lightning. And by definition, all thunderstorms produce lightning. The mountainous terrain of the Rockies contributes to a wealth of thunderstorms. To generate these storms, moisture is a key ingredient. In the Western US, water vapor originates in the Gulf of Mexico, the Gulf of California, and the Pacific Ocean.

The creation of thunderstorms also requires the ingredient of an unstable atmosphere. Large, daily fluctuations in temperature contribute to the necessary instability. Air near the earth's surface absorbs the sun's radiant heat. This warm air then rises to high altitudes, where it runs into cool air, generating increasing instability.

A third necessary ingredient for thunderstorms is a lifting mechanism. The fractured and varied terrain provides this. The upper levels of mountains remain cool year-round, making them ideal retreats from summer heat waves. Lower-level "flatland" heat builds on summer days and soon rises up mountainsides, creating an air movement know as an "upslope condition."

If this rising warm air also contains moisture and encounters a disturbed atmosphere, thunderstorms develop. This formula for storm creation is sometimes described as "mountains generating their own weather."

Lightning Bolts

A bolt of lightning is a giant spark of electricity. Its action heats the surrounding air up to 70,000°F, hotter that the surface of the sun.

This awesome heat causes an explosive expansion of air. It's this explosion that generates the classic thunderclap.

Lightning's electrical spark results from rapidly mixing air currents, which shuffle electrical charges inside a storm. Within a cloud, air normally insulates electrical charges from one another. However, when benign cumulus clouds morph into cumulonimbus clouds, wind updrafts and downdrafts separate positive and negative electrical charges. Positive charges move to the top of the cloud, and negative charges to the bottom. Very powerful electrical fields develop. These fields look for a way to release their charge. When that happens, a zap of lightning occurs.

On a much smaller scale, this is what results when you build up a static charge by walking in wool socks on a wool carpet. Then a small zap occurs when you touch something, such as your dog's wet nose. Backpackers sometimes experience a similar phenomenon on dark nights in a sleeping bag. As you settle in for the night, you can see tiny sparks of light as the different charges in your nylon bag react with each other.

Most lightning occurs between or within clouds and never reaches the earth. This is known as **sheet lightning**. When strikes do occur, it is because, as the storm cloud moves over the ground, the negative charge at the bottom of the cloud is attracted to the positively charged surface of the earth, often connecting to the nearest or highest object. When connection occurs, we see the lightning bolt, which is followed by a peal of thunder.

When Lightning Strikes

We frequently envision a lightning bolt directly striking a hiker or climber. In reality, **direct strikes** are rare. They make up less than 5 percent of lightning fatalities. By far the most common cause of human lightning injury is **ground current**, which is responsible for 50 percent of lightning injuries. Ground currents, as the name implies, result when lightning hits the ground, spreads out in all directions, and travels through the earth.

Lightning has been described as "lazy." It always takes the path of least resistance. Documented examples exist of electricity descending through a tree trunk and then transferring at several feet above ground to descend to the earth through a highly conductive salt-water-filled human being sheltering under the tree.

When lightning does reach the ground, it can travel through tree roots, wet rocks, and crevices in the earth, all of which contain water. Soil moisture and chemical composition can vary the effect. Ground currents have been known to travel several hundred feet from the surface strike, a good reason not to stand near lightning-attracting objects, such as tall trees or poles.

While the main current of a lightning strike generally follows the object it hits into the ground, a phenomenon known as **side flashes** can also occur. This dangerous event sends electricity directly through the air surrounding the point of impact. Unlike ground currents, the voltage of side flashes does not rapidly reduce when traveling though air. Rapidly occurring side flashes are briefly visible and account for up to 35 percent of lightning injuries.

Less common mechanisms of injury from lightning are **upward leaders,** also known as streamers. Responsible for less than 15 percent of injuries, upward leaders are pulses of high current drawn from the earth and seeking to ascend toward incoming lightning strikes. These are highly dangerous to any bystanders.

Thunderstorm Awareness

Thunderstorms and their lightning components are very dangerous to hikers. Include watching for them in your awareness of the environment. If thunderstorms are possible, take steps to prepare for their arrival:

▸ Follow both local and regional weather reports. Note any that cite possible thunderstorms.
▸ Be alert to the arrival of gusty storm fronts. Their leading edge may include thunderstorms.
▸ Heavy raindrops, popcorn-like graupel, or hail stones are often a warning that lightning is soon to follow.
▸ Listen for thunder. It can be heard up to about 10 miles away. Lightning flashes can be seen from longer distances. The sound of thunder travels about a mile every five seconds. You can count time between obvious lightning flashes and obvious bangs. In theory, the closer the two are together, the more danger you are in, and the quicker you need to take precautions. Known as the flash-bang ranging system, it can be a difficult method to apply as you may not be able to tell which flash generated which thunderclap.

▸ Be alert to ominous, dark-black skies or unusual atmospheric events such as St. Elmo's fire, which is a bluish corona discharge, or other unusual colors in the clouds.
▸ Watch and listen for surface events, such as hair standing on end, buzzing metal objects, or crackling or popping noises.
▸ In short, any unusual phenomenon interesting enough to warrant a selfie is your warning to take cover.

LIGHTNING-RISK REDUCTION

In the front country, there are many locations that provide a high level of safety from lightning strikes. Modern buildings are generally very safe locations. They contain internal electrical and plumbing systems that can conduct electricity into their grounded foundations. Stay away from large glass windows where glass contains lead.

Lightning-safety campaigns state, "When thunder roars, go indoors." Heed this good advice and move immediately to shelter as electrical storms approach. When indoors, avoid using computers and other electrical devices, using landline phones, taking baths or showers, and washing dishes, as all these activities can channel electricity. Automobiles with metal tops are a good place of refuge because the steel structure conducts electricity around the occupants. If you shelter in an automobile, avoid touching metal components. In the backcountry, some locations are safer than others, but there is no 100-percent safe location. Outhouses, barns, rustic cabins, tents, lean-tos, and

Lightning striking tallest tree

all-terrain vehicles provide inadequate protection. If you are within a few miles of the trailhead, return to it and seek shelter in a closed vehicle.

- **High-risk locations.** When you observe a thunderstorm approaching, identify and move away from high-risk locations. These include mountain summits, exposed ridgelines, and areas with tall, stand-alone trees or poles. Avoid wet ground, lakes, streams, beaches, islands, and boats. Do not enter caves or mine tunnels unless they are dry and very deep. Wide-open spaces are dangerous, as you may be the highest item around.

- **Low-risk locations.** Western forests tend to be mono-cultures, with few species and a uniform canopy. If such a

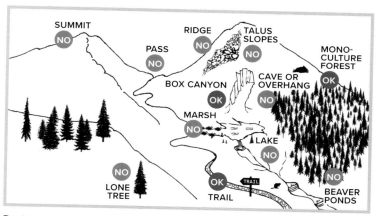

During a thunderstorm, move to a lower-risk location. Illustration by Margaret DeLuca

forest is nearby, move into it. Avoid its tallest trees and any trees showing past lightning damage. Lightning can and does strike twice in the same location. If you are caught descending an open slope, try to stay on the driest ground available. Keep low but do not lie down. Seek a dry gully or ravine.

▸ **If overtaken by lightning.** When it is not possible to move to a safer location and you are exposed, remove rings, watches, metal jewelry, and crampons or microspikes. Lay down trekking poles and ice axes and move away from all metal objects. Have your group spread out as far as possible but at least 50 feet apart and still within sight and sound of each other. The reason for this is that it increases the chance

Lightning positions are a last resort. **Left:** Standing with heels touching **Right:** Better. Low on pad with minimum touching of ground, option if must be in a tent. **Bottom:** Best. Low with only toes touching the ground, eyes closed, ears covered.

that not all individuals will be struck by lightning and thus
can assist those who may have been and also go for help.

The Lightning Position

If a thunderstorm is fully upon you and there is no safe place of
escape, as a last resort, assume the lightning position:

▸ Crouch low with your feet close together. Your heels must
  touch. The theory is that ground-strike lightning, seeking the
  path of least resistance, will travel through one foot and out
  the other, limiting the parts of the body effected.
▸ Try to have as little contact with the ground as possible.
  If you have a foam pad, climbing rope coil, or backpack,
  crouch on it.
▸ Close your eyes to protect them from blinding lightning
  flashes. Cover your ears, as nearby thunderclaps have
  been known to rupture ear drums. Open your mouth to help
  equalize concussive air pressure.

The lightning safety position can be difficult to maintain.
Lightning storms can last thirty minutes. If you tire, sit with your
knees up, feet pointing downhill, and clutch your knees. Use
this latter position if you must be in a tent. Although the insulation value is debatable, sit on your sleeping pad or air mattress.
Do not lie down. Do not touch the sides of the tent or the tent
poles.

AFTER A LIGHTNING INCIDENT

When lightning has moved well away, account for all members of your group. As you check in with each individual, keep in mind that their responsiveness, hearing, and vision may now be impaired.

If individuals are injured, treat those who are unresponsive first. Call 911. Provide CPR to those not breathing and those without a pulse. If you have multiple people needing intervention and cannot treat them all, place unresponsive individuals in the "recovery position," lying them on their side to help avoid choking on any vomit. Check all involved individuals for burns. These may be hidden under clothing.

If your group has just come through a life-threatening thunderstorm, expect members to be wet and cold. Watch for shock, possible amnesia, and developing hypothermia. Lightning may cause internal injuries that are not observable. Signs and symptoms may not show up for several days or weeks. Any member of a group who has been actively involved in a lightning strike, should be seen by a physician at the soonest opportunity.

| **THE REST OF THE STORY . . .** |

Our trip to the summit was slower than anticipated. The scree slopes became slippery and difficult to see in the developing mist. Our "tag" of the summit corresponded with a long, deep, and ominous rumble. The metal stays on my backpack started a maniacal buzzing. No discussion was necessary for both of us to immediately charge back down the ridge we had just ascended.

We descended about 100 yards, when the summit of Holy Cross was rocked by a tremendous explosion. The smell of ozone was unmistakable. Somehow, we found a way to move even faster, as a hailstorm decided to join the fun. Soon, the tree line came into view. Our salvation beckoned. Or so we hoped. The lightning bursts, which had appeared to be slowly pacing themselves, now dramatically upped their tempo. They decided to ignore man's rule that forests are safer locations and began to prune enormous trees on both sides of the trail. Exploding branches and wood splinters leapt into the air all around us. The bombardment seemed to go on forever, as we set personal speed records running down the trail. Eventually, the lightning gods grew tired of educating us. They moved on to torment the pass to the east. And a never-to-be forgotten lesson was learned.

6

Terrain and Pace

I was new to hiking in the West and had just begun to work my way through a list of high mountain peaks. Humboldt Peak (Class 2) in the Sangre de Cristo Range of Colorado was cited as a hikeable mountain. It would provide an orientation to an area populated with numerous, more-challenging peaks. Building a career limited my outdoor time, but a very early Saturday start from my Denver-area home found me at the trailhead by 9:00 a.m. on a beautiful day.

The trail followed an old mining road due west and then turned northeast and ascended the western ridge of Humboldt. I was tired from a stressful work week, the long drive, and lack of sleep. My quart and a half of water was soon gone as I puffed up the rocky trail to the summit. From the mountain ridge, I could see the road on which I'd hiked into the area, weaving through a forest that met the grassy southern flank of Humboldt. On the

87

summit, I studied my topo map. The contour lines on the south slope were further apart (indicating less steep) than those of the western ridge I hiked up. The idea came to me that I could descend the grassy south slopes of Humboldt, bushwhack through the forest, and connect with the lower part of the mining road. My new route was all downhill and should save lots of time, distance, and effort. What a great idea!

Something in my weary brain must have had enough primitive survival energy left to be alarmed at my decision. I heard warning bells go off, but quickly silenced them by asking a very fit-looking couple I met on the summit to let my wife, waiting at the trailhead, know that I had taken a different route back and to look for me descending Humboldt's south slope. With this one small safety step in place, I started down the rocky upper slopes toward the grass meadows. What could go wrong?

ALONG WITH AMPLE BEAUTY AND WONDER, backcountry travel contains its share of risk and danger. As this book details, these can come in many forms: lightning, animal encounters, and forest fires, to name a few. However, the largest source of injury can be directly tied to the act of hiking itself.

National Park Service data lists day hiking and backpacking as the two largest sources of backcountry emergencies. This matches National Forest rescue statistics, which cite hiking as the overwhelming generator of rescue missions. Primarily, hiking incidents relate to travel and terrain issues. Their most common negative outcomes are lower-body sprains, strains, and fractures. Attention to terrain, staying focused while hiking, and having skills in basic hiking technique can go a long way in reducing trip-ending injuries.

PACE

Achieving a steady, efficient, and comfortable pace is a valuable objective. Your goal should be to end the hiking

Humboldt Peak Photo by Jon Kedrowski

day with a reserve of energy available to set up camp, drive home safely, or deal with an emergency.

Hikers are often eager to get out on the trails and so start off at a brisk clip. Two or three hours may pass before they call for a break. Experience suggests a different approach. Instead, plan on taking a quick "gear check" stop about fifteen minutes into your hike. At this point, you will have warmed up and can remove and store excess clothing layers. Tighten your pack straps, adjust boot laces, and judge if any blister-causing hot spots are developing. You will also still be close enough to the trailhead to return for any essential equipment you left behind in the car.

After this first stop, plan on at least one break each hour. Ten minutes is a good maximum, as any longer will allow your

Falls on the Trail

Most backcountry accidents are not fatal, but those that are, are most often related to falling. Technical climbers use sophisticated skills and equipment to protect themselves from likely falls. Their fatality rates are low. Hikers often do not expect dangerous exposure, do not equip for it with climbing gear, and are ill-prepared for dangerous situations.

Key causes and localities of hiking falls include:

▸ Descending low-rated "walk-up" peaks (most accidents occur on descents, not ascents)

▸ Taking selfie photos near cliffs or fall hazards

▸ Edging out onto lookouts for the best photo or view

▸ Cutting switchbacks

▸ Crossing steep snowfields

▸ Crossing bands of "rotten" rock

▸ Descending steep, gravely trails

▸ Crossing high-alpine, Class 3 passes

▸ Hiking trails with exposed tree roots, which become slippery when wet

▸ Overextending and becoming exhausted

muscles to cool and become stiff. Setting regular breaks allows hiking group members to plan how to use their break time efficiently.

Before reaching an anticipated stop, you can develop a mental checklist of things to do during the break. It may include a bathroom break, checking the map, refreshing sunscreen, snacking, and always, hydrating. If each team member follows such a list, no one has to wait for someone who forgot a needed duty. When you start out again, take a look around to make sure nothing has been left behind.

As you settle into a pace, be mindful of your breathing, letting it guide your pace. Ideally, your chosen cadence will allow you to engage in conversations, except perhaps on steep hills or at high altitudes. A group pace should accommodate the slowest hiker. Trips can be ruined if an individual is thoroughly worn out.

If you stop to let a member catch up, do not start out again the moment they join you. Called "slinky hiking," such behavior is easy to slip into, often happens unknowingly, and should be avoided. Give the slowest person a chance to rest and regain energy.

HIKING TECHNIQUES

Hikers can benefit from trekking techniques developed by alpine mountain climbers.

Flat-footed hiking can aid those carrying a heavy pack. Instead of a normal gait, where one steps heel first and then rolls up to the ball of the foot, try walking as the name implies—

flat-footed. This can protect calf muscles and allow you to hike for longer periods of time.

The **rest step**, most often used on steep, high-altitude climbs, can give hikers a lower "gear" and a margin of safety when uphill routes seem never-ending. Practice this skill so you have it in your tool bag if needed. Find a steep, uphill trail or, better yet, a snowfield with firm but not hard snow. Take a forward step and straighten your weight-bearing leg. Lock your knee, exhale, and momentarily pause before you inhale and step onto your other foot. Repeat. Your goal is to relieve leg muscles by briefly resting on your skeletal structure. Hikers complete two exhales and one inhale per step. Climbers at extreme altitudes may take as many as ten or more breaths per step.

Pressure breathing is another mountaineering tool that can assist fatigued mountain hikers. At altitude, there is less atmospheric pressure available to force oxygen molecules into the alveoli of the lungs. A popular but untested theory is that by pursing one's lips and blowing out as if blowing through a small straw, more oxygen is forced into the blood stream. Some climbers may climb an entire high route using this technique and swear by it. It is particularly practical in locations such as Washington state, where climbers live near sea level and journey to nearby high-altitude peaks. Hikers may want to give it a try for a small, needed boost of energy when fatigued or before crossing a challenging section of mountain trail. See if it works for you.

ROCKY MOUNTAIN TERRAIN

In the mountains, a hiker may encounter many types of terrain during a hike. Awareness of and attention to these variations is important.

Scree

Scree is a mass of loose, small rocks that is found on the slopes of young mountain ranges, such as the Rockies. It is also common in volcanic areas. It is made up of rocks ranging from pea-size to tennis-ball-size. Hiking across it can be tedious and dangerous. Seek other routes if you can. If not, try to follow established trails and travel through lower-angle areas, as it can slide.

Scree field Photo by Jon Kedrowski

Hiking up ball-bearing-like scree is difficult and can result in a classic "two steps forward, one step backward" situation. Descending is much easier and involves plunging steps that, with good balance, can carry you several feet with each step. However, scree slopes can also be sensitive ecosystems trying to establish themselves under harsh circumstances. Step on snow patches and larger rocks if you can.

Before tackling a scree area, tighten your boot laces for extra support. If you know you will spend substantial time in such areas, wear gaiters to prevent small rocks from entering your boots.

Talus

Talus refers to fields of rocks larger than scree. The rocks are often angular and sharp. Cross talus fields with care. Some rocks

Talus field

may be covered with colorful primitive scale-like symbiotic orga-nizations called lichen. Lichen-covered rocks usually mean the rocks have settled and are stable. However, in wet weather, lichen become slick and dangerous to walk on.

When encountering talus fields, plan your intended route. Look ahead and choose the best line of travel. Watch for game trails and follow them if available. Entire talus slopes can shift, causing a sort of rock avalanche; one human can be enough to start a slide. If you experience the shifting of more than a few rocks, back out of the area immediately. Helmets are advised in such areas.

Boulder Fields

These fields are areas of large rocks, some of which can be the size of automobiles or larger. They are usually more stable than scree and talus areas. However, if you slip crossing them, your fall may take you down between several rocks. Hikers have become trapped in such situations. Use caution moving from one rock to another. Though large, boulders can be unsettled and tilt when you attempt to cross them. It is a sobering experience to hop on a multi-ton granite boulder and have it wiggle beneath your feet.

Long-established trails through boulder fields typically no longer contain such tippy rocks. If you are approaching a little-used area, stop and prepare. This is a good time for a break, hydration, and a snack. Tighten your shoulder straps, make sure your sternum and waist straps are engaged, and adjust load-riser straps to assure your pack is tight to your back. You want to minimize any shift of your pack that might pull you off balance.

Boulder field

Look before you leap, as the saying goes, and plan your route. Attempt to place your foot on the middle of each rock to minimize shifting. Be nimble and ready to abandon any rock that shifts with your weight. Try for flowing progress as you move from one balanced spot to another, stopping at each to pick your next set of moves.

In fields of smaller rocks, trekking poles can help with balance. Among larger boulders, having your hands free can be an advantage. If you choose to use poles, unstrap your hands, as poles can stick between cracks and pull you off balance.

Falling Rocks

Falling rocks are found in abundance on scree, talus, and boulder fields. It is a humbling experience to watch a large boulder crash down a mountain slope in a cascade of dust, sparks, and

Trekking Poles

Trekking poles are essentially ski poles for summer. They are a great addition to a hiker's safety tool bag. They add stability to crossing rivers, slippery snowfields, and muddy, eroded trails with exposed tree roots. The addition of two more points of contact improves balance when tackling difficult terrain. Using poles engages your upper body muscles and takes weight off your knees. A scientific study reveals that pole use decreased the pressure on knees by 12 to 25 percent.

Poles are made from aluminum or carbon fiber. Carbon fiber is lighter but more expensive. Keep in mind that in an electrical storm, both materials conduct electricity. Collapsible poles have a safety advantage in that you can store them in your pack when you need both hands free for scrambling and rock hopping. Adjustable-length poles allow you to set them at a 90-degree angle to your elbows when hiking on level ground, lengthen them when descending, and shorten them when traveling uphill.

Poles with padding below the grips allow you to quickly grasp poles differentially. This saves time over readjusting poles for each rise and fall of the trail. It is also a helpful feature when hiking across a slope where there is a significant difference between the uphill and downhill side of the trail.

During a rainstorm, using poles may allow water to run into the sleeves of your rain jacket, creating a potential source of wet layers and hypothermia. Stash your poles in your pack during the rain or solve the problem with rain mittens. These lightweight, simple mittens are waterproof and usually not insulated.

shrapnel fragments. The unexpected and unique smell it creates is never forgotten. But it also a dangerous moment. Move across such areas quickly and early in the morning. Rocks are more likely to begin to move in the late morning when sun thaws slopes. If high rockfall activity is observed or expected:

▸ Send your hiking party members across rock fields one at a time.
▸ Position spotters beside the slope with a wide view to warn of falling rocks.
▸ Avoid crossing when other parties are higher up the slope.
▸ If your hiking sets off rockfall or you observe rocks moving, yell "*Rock!*" Keep shouting it until the rock has settled. Do this even if you are not sure whether there is a group below you.
▸ If you hear another hiker shout "*Rock!*" quickly move as close to the rock face as you can. Lean into the slope at the steepest spot available.
▸ If you see the rock coming, visually track it and attempt to move out of its way. Get behind a large boulder if possible.
▸ If you cannot see the approaching rock and cannot lean into the rock face, turn your back to the slope, cover the back of your head with your arms and hope your backpack provides some protection.
▸ Modern climbing helmets are light and comfortable to wear. Bring one along on rock-fall-prone trips.

Snowfields

Snowfields in the Mountain West may be encountered any time of the year. This is especially true on long-distance trails that traverse high mountain passes. Try to time your treks to cross snowy areas in the morning, when snow conditions are likely to be the firmest. Use hiking poles and add snow baskets to them if significant snowfields are expected.

Warmer conditions lead to melting snow, which can lead to icefall and rockfall. When crossing wet, warmed snow, you may "posthole." This is when your feet and legs sink down into the snow, sometimes up to your crotch. Snow will enter your boots and pant legs. Gaiters are invaluable in such conditions. If you don't have gaiters, you can try wrapping a piece of duct tape around your pant cuffs.

Postholing is annoying and tiring and will dramatically slow your travel time. If there are several hikers in your party, rotate taking the lead so that one person isn't doing all the work to break trail.

Be careful along the borders of snowfields. Snow melts quickest and is weakest near the edges. As slopes steepen, you can kick steps into the snow. Try to create stable platforms your hiking partners can also use. Avoid crossing snowfields where a slip will tumble you downhill into rock faces or cliffs. If you must cross such a dangerous snowfield, remove your rain jacket and pants. Their slick surfaces will only make it harder to end a slide if you fall.

Take immediate measures if a slip occurs. Attempt a maneuver mountaineers call "self-arrest," which is an advanced skill.

Self-Arrest with an Ice Axe

If you plan to travel on steep snow, you should carry (and learn to use) an ice axe. This important safety tool looks like a small miners' pick. It can be used for cutting steps and arresting falls. It is best to have formal instruction in its use. Practice self-arrest annually, experimenting with all the positions from which one can fall, for example head high, head low, on your back, on your front. **Select practice locations with gentle, rock-free run-outs.**

Train to use an ice axe

To do this, turn onto your stomach and move your head uphill. Grasp your hands in front of you, dig your elbows into the snow and attempt to slow yourself by gathering snow between your arms. At the same time, spread your legs, raise your seat, and dig in your toes.

An immediate reaction is critical. Speed builds quickly in a fall and can become impossible to overcome. Practice this activity yearly on snow slopes with a safe runout. Your goal is for this exercise to become instinctive. (See the "Sage Advice" section, previous page, for tips on the advanced skill of self-arrest using an ice axe.)

Plunge-stepping is an efficient way to descend a snowy slope quickly. Facing downhill, hop from foot to foot, taking turns plunging your heel through the crust of the snow. Keep your "nose over your toes" and bend at the waist. Keep your knees slightly bent. (This is effective on scree slopes too.)

Under the correct conditions, sliding downhill on your boots, known as glissading, is a fun alternative. The correct conditions are firm snowfields with an ample rock-free runout, should you lose your balance. Here, with good balance, you can slide downhill using your boots as if they were skis. On steep slopes, it is best to carry an ice axe in a ready position, with both hands holding the axe across the chest, available for immediate use. If you are wearing old trousers or rain pants, you can also glissade on your backside. Never glissade wearing microspikes or crampons.

TRAVELING CROSS-COUNTRY (OFF-TRAIL)

Cross-country, or off-trail travel is sometimes a necessary and sometimes a voluntary form of backcountry hiking. But it is always an adventure! It is also known as bushwhacking, named after the likelihood that you will be "whacked" by bushes when you attempt it. Going cross-country is an advanced hiking skill and not for beginners. One needs strong map and compass training, and advanced "lost-proofing" skills to accomplish it safely.

Bushwhacking skills are useful if your hike purpose requires travel off established trails. This might include seeking an obscure peak, scouting an alpine lake for a backcountry fishing experience, or seeking out invasive species of plants for eradication treatments during a wilderness-area volunteer project.

As visitation to public lands has increased crowding, hikers have learned that off-trail travel can lead to areas of solitude and beauty. In bushwhacking, you are not traveling to get to a naturally beautiful location. Rather, you are immersed in it as soon as you step off the trail. You will confront terrain without the advantage of graded paths and switchbacks. And you will discover hidden wilderness gems of old growth forests, secluded campsites, meadows of wildflowers untrampled by humans, and amazing geologic formations. You will also find increased biodiversity and abundant wildlife that exists away from human-frequented areas.

The aesthetic and personal rewards of cross-country travel are high. So are the risks. Your chances of becoming bewildered and lost increase. Your route will be full of fallen timber, ankle-twisting rocks, spiderwebs stretched between bushes, and uneven footing. Timbered areas will inevitably poke you in the forehead or eyes. And meadows that appear dry will surprise you by soaking your boots.

Prepare well for cross-country travel. Follow the lost-proofing procedures found in this book (see Chapter 9). You will be far from other humans and emergency assistance. If you become incapacitated, how will you obtain help?

Expect travel to be double your typical trail times. While trails have been routed around physical barriers, going cross-country

Bushwhacking Fashion

Don't wear your finest hiking clothes unless it's a backcountry wedding. It is best to wear long-sleeved shirts and to avoid shorts when bushwhacking. Gloves are useful as well. Hunters who frequently travel cross-country often wear heavy-duty, thorn-proof clothing. In dense forest areas, you typically look down to watch your footing and are commonly struck in the head by branches, some of which can be very sharp. Wear a hat and sunglasses or other eye protection. If you are ascending through tree line to reach a peak climb and have a climbing helmet with you, put it on. You will be amazed at how many times you hear amplified scrapes and clunks from the helmet brushing against tree limbs. Leave plenty of room between hikers so branches don't snap back at your partners.

Hiking Etiquette

Trail right of way sign

Hiking trail etiquette is similar in purpose to social etiquette with your friends, family, and coworkers. These voluntary rules make the outdoor experience more pleasant and fun for everyone. In many cases, they also make it safer.

Start with courtesy toward others on the trail. A friendly attitude goes a long way. Most trails are multiuse. Expect horses, bikes, runners, dogs, and llamas.

▶ Horses and other pack stock have the primary right of way. They are the least maneuverable in small trail areas and can be unpredictable. If you are carrying a large backpack or fishing rod, you do not present the shape of a regular human being. This can startle a horse. Move downhill, off the path and talk calmly to the horse, so it knows you are a person.

▶ Hikers are next on the list, with bikers called on to yield to them by the International Mountain Biking Association guidelines and most park regulations. The rational here is bikes are considered more maneuverable and thus better able to avoid hikers. However, most hikers usually welcome a short break to let bikers pass. Most bikers announce themselves and are courteous. The annoying small percentage who blast past without a word of warning are often newbies who don't know better.

▶ Hikers must yield to other hikers. Those going uphill have the right of way. This is based on safety, as hikers ascending have a smaller field of vision than those descending.

▶ When passing another trail user, try not to startle that person or animal. A friendly "hi" is a welcome gesture that adds to a positive day outdoors.

▶ Be mindful of trail conditions. Avoid muddy, wet trails, usually found in springtime. If you find yourself on a muddy or wet trail, always walk through it, rather than expanding the path by walking on its shoulder.

▶ You will encounter wildlife. Animals have learned that the trails made by humans are energy-saving ways to cover distance. Try not to disturb animals and never get too close. Do not feed them.

▶ Most trail authorities are underfunded. The US Forest Service has undergone decades of reduction of its trail-maintenance budget. If you encounter a recently dropped tree limb, move it to the downhill side of the trail. Do not move large, downed trees, as they are sometimes torqued from their fall and can be dangerous.

▶ Report trail damage to park and forest authorities. Mobile apps can be a quick, efficient way to do so. Learn to use mobile apps, such as the Colorado Mountain Club's Recreation Impact Monitoring System (RIMS) or various electronic data-reporting forms maintained by the Forest Service and allied volunteer support organizations.

may lead you directly into them. If this happens, use your compass to take a 90-degree turn from your intended route. Count your steps, and when to the side of the barrier, take another 90-degree turn back to your original heading. Walk that direction until around the obstruction. Make a third 90-degree turn and take the same number of steps you walked in the opposite direction. This maneuver will return you to your original bearing, where you can make a final 90-degree turn back on your route.

Going down grassy, steep slopes can appear benign, but they become deadly when wet. Be especially careful where fall potential exists. View them as Class 4 climbs and use solid handholds or rope assists.

Downhill walking is strenuous. Most hiking, backpacking, and mountaineering accidents occur on downhill trails and during descents from climbing objectives. Classic examples known to SAR teams are hikers caught above tree line in lightning storms who then ran downhill toward the safety of tree line. Muscles weary from uphill trail sections and the momentum of descent can make for spectacular falls.

Downhill walking is tedious and can be especially difficult off-trail. The weight of a heavy pack tries to pull you backward when descending. Your balance is affected, and your feet want to slide out in front of you. Focus is important. Shorten your stride going downhill. Small steps are best. Bend your knees and try to step heel first, rather than toe first. Lengthen adjustable trekking poles for extra downhill reach.

Boot size is important. Boots that are too small are especially annoying. Toes tend to jam against the front of the boot and cause blood blisters and blackened nails. Hikers and mountaineers are often recognized by cases of "climber's toe." Try to limit downhill damage by applying Vaseline or a body glide product to toes and lacing boots tightly before descent. A high point, summit, or ridge can be a good place to change into spare dry socks for the downward trip.

THE REST OF THE STORY . . .

The first sign of something wrong was as I descended from talus onto the grassy slopes of Humboldt. Only, the slopes were not made up of grass. Instead, they were a slippery combination of alpine plants, sagebrush, and clumps of wildflowers. Beautiful, but hard to walk on. Despite traveling downhill, my progress was slowed by the need to step carefully on the uneven terrain. The best progress was made by creating my own switchbacks, an effort that quickly wore out the leg that was uphill at the time.

In this annoying and tiring fashion, I descended several thousand feet. By now, it was clear my route was a bad idea. I realized I should be wise and climb back to the summit-ridge trail. However, the tree line was getting nearer, and all would soon be better. Only, it was not. The tree line and thick forest were bordered on the uphill side by 50- to 100-foot cliffs, invisible from above. I wandered the cliff edge looking for safe places to descend. There were none. I was experiencing the infamous condition of being "cliffed out." Evening was fast approaching. I could not go down, and reclimbing to the summit was beyond my diminished strength.

I sat on the steep cliff edge, able to see my target destination, the miner's road, but it might as well have been miles away. Near my perch, a lofty fir tree rose ramrod straight 60 feet up from the forest floor at the cliff base and about 10 feet out from me. Its top branch was a few feet below my seat. I had recently seen an old movie where action hero Charles Bronson escaped murderous pursuers in exactly the same situation, by leaping off a cliff face into a treetop. My foggy brain did not identify that he likely had a stunt double who had numerous safety ropes attached and his tree was green Styrofoam.

I now knew my next move. I had seen Forest Service smoke-jumper films in which firefighters parachuted into thick forests. They wore special padded suits to help them descend through sharp tree branches. I duplicated their apparel as best I could by putting on all my extra clothes and rain suit. I took a deep breath, and then I jumped. Two surprising experiences then occurred. First, I landed safely in the treetop and had wrapped my arms and legs around the trunk. Second, I learned that it takes a very long time to climb down a 60-foot-tall fir tree, certainly much longer than it took Charles Bronson's stunt double. P.S. I never told my wife this story.

Note: Hopefully, you have realized I am a bad example, and you should never try this!

7

Altitude

Three friends who had met in high school thought it would be a great way to reunite. One buddy would fly to Colorado from the Midwest and join the others, who now lived in the Centennial State. Together, they would climb Fairview Peak (13,000 feet) in the Never Summer Range. Fairview was the name of their Ohio high school, and it would be fun to take summit photos wearing Fairview High School athletic gear. Over the years, the three had hiked and climbed together. The Colorado residents suggested time should be taken to acclimate, but their Ohio friend assured them he ran a lot and was in great shape. They picked him up at Denver Airport and after one night in Boulder, headed to a mountain basecamp. Spirits and hopes were high!

Western States High Points

The Rocky Mountain region is also known as the "High West." And with good reason. The Western states contain some of the highest altitude peaks in the Western Hemisphere, most of which are hikeable.

Arizona	Humphreys Peak	12,633'
California	Mount Whitney	14,494'
Colorado	Mount Elbert	14,433'
Idaho	Borah Peak	12,662'
Montana	Granite Peak	12,799'
Nevada	Boundary Peak	13,140'
Oregon	Mount Hood	11,239'
Utah	Kings Peak	13,528'
Washington	Mount Rainier	14,410'
Wyoming	Gannett Peak	13,804'

Much of the Western U.S. is at high altitude.

STATES IN AMERICAN'S WEST are home to some of the loftiest altitudes in the country. In this region, popular hiking locations are located in national forests and parks, which often encompass elevated terrain. Hiking mountain trails, crossing high mountain passes, and "peak bagging" are increasingly popular activities.

ALTITUDE SICKNESS

Once you are above 4,000 feet in altitude, physiological changes occur in your body. This is the result of decreased atmospheric pressure. Less air pressure can lead to insufficient blood oxygen levels. It is air pressure that diffuses oxygen into the alveoli of your lungs and into your blood. The higher you travel, the less oxygen enters your blood stream.

Acute Mountain Sickness (AMS)

Functional complications start to occur around 8,000 feet. As your body works to respond to oxygen deficiency, various symptoms may be present. The most common are headaches but also dizziness, nausea, vomiting, low energy, and loss of appetite can occur. This least-serious altitude illness is known as acute mountain sickness (AMS) and is linked to your brain. AMS is most common in individuals who have recently traveled from lower altitudes. The classic case is a skier who recently flew from a sea-level city and immediately departed the airport for a mountain resort. As many as one in four such travelers contract AMS. The good news is your body will eventually adapt to higher elevations

Altitude warning

through the process known as acclimatization. This adaption can take a few days or up to several months.

An early adaptation occurs to your breathing. The depth and rate of respiration increases, causing more oxygen to enter the alveoli and more carbon dioxide to be expelled. This process leads to increased alkalinity, which in turn causes the kidneys to excrete bicarbonate into the urine. Diuresis (increased discharge of urine) occurs as the body attempts to eliminate these fluids. Your heart will beat more quickly in an attempt to deliver additional oxygen.

With time, red blood cell levels increase, and your heart and muscles become more efficient. The progression of these adaptations is related to individual differences and personal metabolism. Those most at risk are young, female hikers who ascended quickly and have a prior history of AMS.

With rest, mild AMS usually resolves itself in a day or two. If it does not, descent will improve the situation. Severe AMS can include fluid in the lungs, declining mental status, and the inability to breathe regularly at rest. Individuals with severe AMS must descend 2,000 to 4,000 feet immediately.

High-Altitude Pulmonary Edema (HAPE)

Edema is swelling caused by excess fluid trapped in your body's tissues. HAPE is a serious condition and less common than AMS. HAPE is the cause of the most altitude-related deaths. Usually occurring above 10,000 feet, it involves significant fluid build-up in the lungs. Patients exhibit blue or gray lips, a feeling of suffocation, and a persistent productive cough of a white frothy fluid. Immediate descent of 2,000 to 4,000 feet is mandatory, as is medical treatment.

High-Altitude Cerebral Edema (HACE)

Typically occurring above 13,000 feet (but could be as low as 10,000 feet), HACE is a dangerous, life-threatening condition. If untreated, death occurs due to the swelling of brain tissue from

OXYGEN AVAILABILITY	FEET	OXYGEN
Sea level	0'	100%
Denver, Colorado *The Mile High City*	5,280'	82%
Mount Whitney, California *Highest point in lower United States*	14,494'	59%
La Rinconada, Peru *Highest settlement in the world*	16,732'	55%
Denali, Alaska *Highest point in North America*	20,310'	47%
Mount Everest, Nepal *Highest point in the world*	29,032'	33%

fluid leakage. Patients display loss of coordination and balance (ataxia), decreasing levels of responsiveness, irritability, and vomiting. Immediate descent is required, as is advanced medical treatment.

Descend, Descend, Descend

If altitude-related issues continue, do not hesitate to take rest days, which can allow your body to catch up with the higher altitude. They also allow extra sleep, a proven aid to acclimatization. If symptoms persist or if HACE or HAPE is present, it is important to rapidly descend. The patient should not descend alone, Descent of at least 2,000 to 4,000 feet is critical.

SAGE ADVICE

Acclimatize

If you are new to the higher elevation of the High West, approach the difference with respect. Acclimatization will progress due to your rapid breathing during day hikes. It will decline during sleep when slow, autonomic functions take over. Counter nighttime's slow acclimatization by sleeping at a lower altitude, at least 1,000 feet below where you plan to hike. If you have a multiday trip planned, you can improve your adaptation by visiting locations over 9,000 feet at least two times in the month before your trip.

In all cases of altitude illness, follow the advice of wilderness medicine practitioners. Their direction is that the three most important treatments are:

1. Descend.
2. Descend.
3. Descend!

THE REST OF THE STORY . . .

Due to a late evening of laughter and catching up, the friends' start the next morning was later than hoped for. However, the skies were blue, and not a cloud was in sight. All went well until the last 500 feet to the summit. At this point, the friend from Ohio shared that he was dizzy and having balance problems. Nevertheless, he was determined to summit and did so. But he was clearly suffering and could barely stand for the summit photos. Time on the peak was quickly cut short, and the group descended. Their stricken companion was swaying and tilting as his partners held his belt and guided him safely back to the trailhead, where a review of a first aid book confirmed a clear case of AMS and ataxia. This was resolved by rest, hydration, and a drive down to Denver.

8

The Ten Essentials

I knew we were in immediate trouble. Becca and I had finally climbed out of the narrow gully containing a stream that flowed from high-altitude Chihuahua Lake. We now had a clear view to the west, and that view was filled with enormous black monsoon thunderheads rapidly moving toward us.

Becca (not her real name) was a new student in the CMC Backpacking School. The students were on their first backpacking field trip, and for most, it was their first night ever camping out. Students and instructors had hiked into the valley below that morning and set up tents. After lunch and navigation instruction, the group set out for an afternoon 5-mile, round-trip hike. I was an instructor and volunteered to stick with Becca when it became clear that, despite being highly motivated, she could not keep up with the other students.

We had often hiked this route in previous classes, and it was protocol that all students and instructors regrouped at the lake for snacks and water refills before heading down a different trail and back to camp. Today, no one else was in sight when Becca and I arrived. Upon seeing the rapidly approaching storm, the instructors had most likely and wisely moved their groups immediately downhill to escape the very exposed lake plateau. We were alone.

I tried to be as positive and calm as I could be as I explained to Becca the steps to take in a lightning storm and to prevent exposure. I told her she was going to get her money's worth of a full mountain experience: hail, high winds, rain, and lightning. I told her we would move as fast as we could, I would not leave her, and we would put on warm layers and our rain gear when we felt the first raindrop.

The first blast of the storm arrived in the form of high winds and graupel, soft popcorn-like balls of hail. Becca rapidly dressed head to toe in her rain gear. I put on my rain pants and reached for my rain parka. Earlier in the day, I had tied it to the outside of my pack. It was now nowhere to be found. Becca could not find her way back without me, and without a rain jacket, I was likely to soon fall prey to hypothermia.

THE CHOICE OF GEAR to take on a hiking trip is a personal one. A hiker needs to balance factors such as weight, expected weather, comfort, availability, and expense. The outdoor industry produces an overwhelming array of gadgets and devices from which to choose, making it difficult to know what to carry.

Fortunately, when safety is the parameter being considered, an almost universally acknowledged list of essential gear has evolved. Carrying the items specified will go a long way toward ensuring you can respond to an emergency or accident. You will be able to safely spend an unplanned night out and also be in a position to assist other, less-prepared travelers.

THE TEN ESSENTIALS

The Ten Essentials list was first created by the Seattle-based Mountaineers hiking club in the 1930s. It is now widely accepted internationally and is documented to have saved numerous lives. Many permutations of it have evolved. You will hear of the "12 Essentials," the "Ten Essentials Plus," the "Survival Essentials," and others. The Mountaineers updated the list in 2010 to encompass a "systems approach." They now look beyond a list of specific items to carry to a list of functional systems that respond to critical needs. Their list is:

1. Navigation
2. Sun protection
3. Insulation (extra clothing)
4. Illumination
5. First aid supplies
6. Fire starter

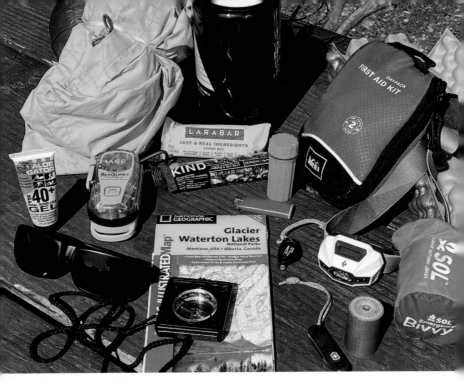

The Ten Essentials

7. Repair kit and tool, including knife
8. Nutrition (extra food)
9. Hydration (extra water)
10. Emergency shelter

A useful list, developed by CMC Master Instructor Steve Billig, adapted the Ten Essentials list to fit the memorable acronym SSNNIIFFR (pronounced "sniffer"): shelter, sun protection, navigation, nutrition/hydration, insulation, illumination, first aid, fire starter, and repair kit and tools. Communication has since been added as an additional item. When heading out for the trail, think of SSNNIIFFR-C to remind you of the contents you should have in your pack. Let's take a closer look at each.

1. Shelter

Backpackers plan for nights out and routinely carry tents with them. Day hikers, however, do not expect to be out overnight and typically do not bring a tent they are unlikely to use. In the past, essential lists have not included shelter. But in recent years, the Mountaineers added shelter to their seminal list. This represents improvements in technology, such as lightweight shelters that now make it both practical and wise for day hikers to carry them. Bivy sacks are one- or two-person sleeping-bag-shaped tubes of thin material that are closed on one end. Typically made of waterproof nylon, these allow you to climb in to escape windy, wet, or cold weather. Ultralight emergency bivies made of polyethylene now exist and should be on every hiker's essentials list.

Bargain Essentials

Assembling the Ten Essentials can be costly. Check out Appendix A for advice on a less-expensive route that will get you started.

A rudimentary bivy sack can be made from two large black trash sacks. Heavy-duty contractor bags work best. Tarps are also lightweight and can be used as emergency shelters. Heavy-duty space blankets, with a silver heat-reflective side, also work well. If you go this route, buy one that has a bright-orange side. It will allow the tarp to draw attention. Avoid red tarps, which are hard to see in dark forests. Add nylon cord to any tarp's corner grommets, so you have guy lines to erect the tarp and do not have to attach them during an emergency.

2. Sun Protection

The Mountain West is the home of high altitude and intense ultraviolet rays. Sunglasses, sunscreen, and hats are key. Sunglasses will protect you from debilitating blindness, especially in snowfields. Wrap-around styles work best. Seek glasses with a visible light transmission (VLT) of between 5 and 20 percent. Sunscreen is also important in mountain travel. Select one with at least a sun protection factor (SPF) of 30 and make sure it protects from both ultraviolet A (UVA) and ultraviolet B (UVB) rays. Choose a broad-brim hat with a dark-colored under-brim and a chin strap.

3. Navigation

The most basic and durable navigation tools are a physical map and compass—and the ability to use them. These will keep you on track and are important tools for pinpointing your location if you are lost. There will be times when you swear your compass is wrong and the earth's magnetic field has been altered. A trap you can easily fall into is imagining the map fits the topography you are seeing, when in reality, it does not. This is called "bending the map." Here a backup compass is invaluable to reassure you that your compass is correct. An inexpensive, simple compass, such as those on keychain whistles or thermometers, will serve you well as a backup. You may also have a compass utility in your cell phone or on your field watch. A GPS unit is valuable but, along with the cell phone, is breakable and subject to drained batteries.

4. Nutrition/Hydration

Your goal is to have extra food and water beyond what you need for a one-day hike. Usually, two to three liters of water is adequate for a hike. Lightweight iodine pills, such as Potable Aqua, are an excellent backup that can purify water you refill in the field. Electrolyte packets will provide some electrolytes, vitamins, and improved taste to water refills. Extra nutrition can take the form of sports bars, energy gels, or hard candy, which travel well. Ideally, you will end each day hike with the extra food in your pack.

5. Insulation

On a day hike, it is not your intention to spend the night. However, just in case, you should take enough extra clothes to survive the coldest expected overnight temperature. A lightweight down coat appropriate for the season is a good choice, as are gloves and an extra pair of socks. A watch cap (beanie) should always travel in your pack. A rain jacket and rain pants are mandatory. Ideally, buy rain pants with side zippers, which allow you to easily put them on without taking off your footwear. Avoid lightweight ponchos, which can be problematic in mountain winds.

Few backpacks are waterproof. Snow will find its way into your pack on winter hikes, usually on breaks. Carry extra clothing in a waterproof bag, such as the ones river runners use. Choose a bright color, which will make it easy to find in the bottom of a dark pack.

6. Illumination

If you carry a flashlight, choose one that is flat and plastic. You can hold it in your teeth, freeing your hands for camp tasks. A far better choice is a head lamp. It turns with your gaze and leaves your hands free. Carry spare batteries. For a backup light, consider a small clip (pinch) light. Always store your lights in the same place in your pack, so you can find them by feel in the dark of night.

7. First Aid

Only carry the first aid materials you know how to use. A basic, commercially made kit is a good way to start. Augment it with personal items and a three-day supply of any prescription you require. A condensed first aid guide is an excellent addition to your kit. Refresh your kit before each trip. See Appendix B for a suggested list of basic first aid items.

8. Fire Starter

Carry two methods to ignite an emergency fire. A butane lighter and waterproof, self-striking matches in a medicine bottle, to protect them from moisture, are a good combination. Also critical is a fire starter—some sort of highly flammable material that ignites easily and burns hot enough and long enough to start wet kindling burning. Packets of military trioxane, purchased at a surplus store, or cotton balls coated with Vaseline and stored in a zipper bag will serve well as fire starters. In a pinch, you can use lip balm or even the corn chips in your lunch sack.

9. Repair Kit and Tools

A small pocketknife with a few incorporated tools works well. Hefty Bowie-type knives are rarely necessary. Duct tape is always valuable for repairing clothing rips, holes in tarps, or treating blister-causing footwear hot spots. Some lightweight rope is a good

Gear Storage

SAGE ADVICE

It takes time and thought to reassemble your essential items before each trip. Keep small items together in a dedicated waterproof ditty bag—I use one that is nylon on one side and clear plastic on the other so I can easily see and find a needed item. If you use a variety of packs (expedition pack, summit pack, winter pack, daypack, or others), you can easily move your essentials to the pack you are using and not have to reassemble the items for each trip. See-through plastic bins are handy for storing your large gear items between trips.

addition for building an emergency shelter, replacing broken boot laces, or hanging a bear bag.

10. Communication

Communication tools are key. At the minimum, carry a whistle. Whistles can be heard at longer distances than the human voice. See Appendix C for a Sample Whistle Protocol. Avoid metal whistles and those with internal balls as these are likely to freeze in winter. Other worthwhile communication tools include cell phones, personal locator beacons, and satellite communicators.

The Essentials Plus

There are some items that do not make the top Ten Essentials list but are close runners-up and worth carrying.

Closed-Cell Foam Pad. This type of pad provides great insulation for little weight. Cut a piece to fit inside your pack on the side toward your back. It takes little space, will provide extra padding for your back, and will be there if you need it to protect you from the cold ground.

Insect Repellant. You can survive overnight without insect repellant, but your life will be much happier if you have it. Plus, increasing numbers of mosquitoes, ticks, and biting flies carry insect-borne diseases.

Garbage Bags

Large black plastic garbage bags can serve many survival purposes:

1. Cut a head-sized hole in the closed end to make an emergency rain jacket.

2. Fill with dry leaves to make an insulated bed.

3. Fill with green vegetation, leave in the sun with the closed end lower than the top, and it will generate drinking water.

4. Fill with snow and place in the sun on a slope, and meltwater will collect.

5. Line your backpack with a bag to keep contents dry.

6. Place over your pack as a rain cover.

7. Slide into one for an emergency bivy.

Trash bag bivy Photo by Frank Bursynski

Toilet Kit. This kit adds to your comfort and sanitation and is becoming more important as there is an expanding use of our public lands. Carry an alcohol-based hand sanitizer (which also works well as a fire starter), toilet paper, a digging tool, and disposal bags. At lower altitudes, you may be able to bury feces and have it decompose, but never at higher altitudes. Always carry out feces and toilet paper in designated disposal bags, also called blue bags or WAG (waste alleviation and gelling) bags.

Chemical Hand Warmers. These packets can provide hours of comfort in cold-related emergency situations. They seem to work best if kept warm in a jacket pocket or pack before they are needed.

Flagging Tape. Also known as surveyors tape, this plastic one-inch tape comes in rolls and a variety of colors. Select a bright one, such as day-glow orange. Cut off a dozen three-foot sections, make mini roles, and secure with tape. They will prove invaluable for marking sketchy trail junctions, affixing to your pack for visibility during hunting season, and marking return routes on climbing scrambles or obscure trail junctions. You can even write messages on the tape and leave route information for searchers if you become lost.

THE REST OF THE STORY . . .

All backcountry hikers are encouraged to carry the Ten Essentials. In the bottom of my pack was a large black plastic garbage bag. I quickly cut a slot for my head in the sealed end and two slots for my arms in the sides. My new, improvised rain jacket worked amazingly well. My arms got wet, but my core remained warm and dry. Becca and I slowly made it back to camp in the dark and rain, tired but with a new adventure on the books and ready for a hot dinner. Even freeze-dried food would taste good this night.

9

Staying Found

DON'T LET THIS HAPPEN TO YOU

It is four months into my semi-retirement, and I am finally doing something I had promised myself I would do for years. When I worked full time, my wilderness travel was restricted to long weekends, spring breaks, and annual vacations. I saved those precious days for climbing most of the 100 tallest Colorado peaks, going on group backpacking trips, and visiting national parks. During drives to those landmark destinations, I spotted other interesting valleys and mysterious canyons. I promised myself when I retired and had unlimited time, I would return and explore these little-visited areas.

It's late in the day, and I have been following an old, unmarked social trail along a mountain creek, as it heads through Douglas fir and aspen forest. My steady hiking rhythm has lulled me into an almost hypnotic reverie. This lack of focus comes to a dramatic end when I realize I am no longer on a trail. A feeling of dread creeps in and I realize I am lost.

IF YOU SPEND ENOUGH TIME in the outdoors, chances are that on occasion, you will find yourself lost. At best, it is a panic-producing situation and at worst, a life-threatening event.

In remote backcountry areas, which are among the most challenging of locations, it is possible to become lost even a short distance from a road or trailhead. Hunters spot game from a road and hastily pursue it into trailless vegetation. They are focused on their prey and neglect to mark their bushwhacking route. Cross-country runners are watching their footing and fail to see forks in the trail. Hikers become confused by several trails that depart from a single trailhead. In all cases, being lost is a traumatic experience.

LOST-PROOFING

Lost-proofing involves steps taken prior to a hike that dramatically improve your chances of staying found. Try these steps to help lost-proof your next wilderness trip.

Do Your Planning Homework

Half the fun of a trip can be its anticipation. Find your proposed trip in a trail guidebook and learn about its characteristics. Authors will often provide trip distance, elevation gain, key landmarks,

Hiking guidebooks abound. Photo by Mary Bradley

water sources, and potential campsites. Typically, route maps are included and increasingly GPS waypoints are as well. Guidebooks commonly assign difficulty rankings to various trails, and you can pick one that matches your ability. Photocopy the pages describing your chosen trail. Carry them with you in double-bagged food storage bags. Make two sets: one to keep handy as you hike and a second set in the bottom of your pack as a backup.

A quick online search will yield dozens of quality trail guides for specific communities, parks, or regions. On a rainy day, they are a great way to daydream about trips to add to your bucket list.

Planning can also include reviewing your proposed route on electronic trail guides. An increasing array of navigation applications are available for smartphones. If your planned trail is a popular one, you can usually find it on one of these apps, and the content usually discusses trail characteristics. These guides often have GPS links so you can chart your trail progress and present location. Some apps allow you to fly over your proposed terrain. They often are three-dimensional and use actual aerial photography.

These apps are excellent tools for staying found or locating your position if lost. Their weakness occurs in that the several satellite signals needed may not be available in canyon terrain or dense forest. As they are also vulnerable to depleted batteries or breakage, they serve best as backup devices to traditional map-and-compass navigation.

While trail guides focus specifically on your chosen route, it is helpful to also have a big-picture sense of the area in which you intend to hike. Regional maps covering an entire area or park serve this purpose. This will enable you to understand where other trails connect with your chosen route as well as to have some information concerning what is over the horizon. These guides highlight the various land management entities and parks you may be passing through. Knowing this, you can consult rangers or websites for current trail conditions and travel alerts. If you get in trouble on a trip, being aware of whose jurisdiction you are in can speed rescue.

Trails Illustrated maps, by National Geographic, are a good choice. Maps are designed for a specific purpose, such as highway travel or aviation. National Geographic maps are designed for hikers and outdoor recreationists. They are topographical

Trails Illustrated maps. Photo by Frank Biasi/National Geographic

maps, which show landscape features, such as cliffs, streams, lakes, and forests. They emphasize county, forest, and park boundaries, which are key landmarks in backcountry navigation. No map is perfect, but Trails Illustrated maps are regularly updated and field verified. Geological features rarely change, but trails are occasionally rerouted, so you will want the most up-to-date map edition available. If your travels are overnight, spend time reviewing your maps before you head out each morning.

Leave a Trace

Always let someone know where you are going and when you expect to return. Fill out a Leave a Trace Trip Plan, such as the example in Appendix D, and leave it with a trusted individual who will call for help if you have not contacted them by a designated time. You should include an extra margin of time in case you run into unexpected but not dangerous delays. Also, it is not uncommon to complete your hike, go to check in, and find you are out of cell phone range.

Know what land management jurisdiction you plan to be in, for example *Manti-La Sal National Forest, San Juan County, Utah*. Leave the phone number your friend should call to report your absence. The form contains information your caller should share with the responding agency, such as the license plate number and description of the vehicle you are using, the name and location of the trailhead, and the planned route you are taking. Leave as much detail as you can about the gear you are carrying, the color of your parka and backpack, and your skill level.

Instruct your friend to stay close to the phone after they have called for help and to expect numerous calls from responding agencies. Share with your friend the possibility they might have to repeat the information several times to different agencies. If possible, before you start your hike, send your friend an electronic photo of you at the trailhead in your gear, which they can share with responding agencies.

Be Aware at the Trailhead

Park your car engine out. This helps a lot if you return to a dead battery and need a jump or critters decide to chew key motor parts. Before you leave your car, check that you have all your gear. Place items left behind under car seats or otherwise out

Always check the trailhead kiosk.

of sight. Clip your car keys inside a pack pocket or keep them securely zipped into a clothing pocket. Be very deliberate in remembering where you put them. Drivers should let others in the hiking party know where the car keys are located.

Be situationally aware and take a tour of the parking lot. Note who your traveling companions on the trail might be. Stickers and license plates will give you lots of clues. Bow-hunter stickers tell you it is archery season. SAR stickers may mean a rescue is occurring. Stickers from hiking clubs or for nature causes also offer clues about the kinds of individuals you will be sharing the

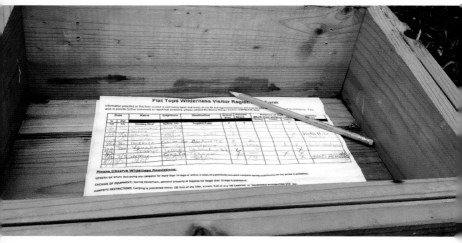

Always sign in at trail registration boxes.

trail with. Governmental license plates alert you to the possibility of rangers or forest workers on the trail.

Study any trailhead kiosk information and read all postings. Be sure to take note of any notices or warnings that other hikers may have posted about trail conditions or animal encounters. Back up your paper map by taking a cell phone photo of any posted trail map. Also take a photo of signs located near the trailhead that list distances to various trail junctions. And don't forget to snap that photo of yourself to send to your trusted contact (assuming you have cell service).

Registration boxes are often located a short way up the trail. Always sign any provided trip registration forms. If the forms are missing or completely full, leave your own note or business card with the date and start time. These boxes are checked by SAR individuals and can provide valuable information if you are lost.

Before you start up the trail, find the trailhead location on your map. Circle it for a quick reference guide. Orient your map and anticipate the first major landmark you will pass on the trail. Note the time you started and check the altitude. Double-check you have all your gear. Check to see if there is cell phone reception at the trailhead. That can be important knowledge to have in an emergency.

Orient the Group

When you are in a group, it is wise to review your hiking plans at the trailhead. How often will you take breaks? What is your target destination? When will you turn around?

Groups are often friends and know each other's skills and abilities. They cooperate and communicate in an informal manner. Larger groups would do well to be more systematic in assigning leadership. Ideally, the group would designate a trip leader. Another helpful role is a designated rear leader, who can communicate with the leader and ensure no one straggles behind.

Leadership duties in such groups are often very informal but predetermining leadership becomes valuable in the event of an emergency. Having a designated leader facilitates decision-making and clarity should an incident occur. At the trailhead, it is also wise to determine if any members have medical training.

Groups should work to stay together. Stretching out, with fast members pushing ahead and slower members falling behind, is a significant cause of lost hikers. On some group hikes, the trip proceeds at the pace of the slowest hikers. As you can imagine, this could make for challenges and frustrations, and it is why trip difficulty rankings are developed and posted before many organized outings. Members can attach themselves to groups of similar ability, thus avoiding disharmony generated by those of widely varying abilities.

STAYING-FOUND NAVIGATION

Sound navigation skills are a great asset for safe travel in backcountry areas. Formal training is available online from major outdoor clubs, such as the Colorado Mountain Club, the Appalachian Mountain Club, and the Mountaineers. This should be reinforced with practice in the field. Outdoor time enhances learning by allowing one to compare the colored lines on a map with actual cliffs, rivers, and foot trails.

Mastering navigation techniques is very worthwhile but beyond the scope of this book. What follows are basic map and compass techniques critical to the purpose of staying found. They can keep you on track as you build more advanced skills.

Study the Route

Before you head out, study your intended route on your map. The best maps for hikers are those designed for recreational purposes (such as National Geographic's Trails Illustrated maps).

Spend time reading the content provided on the border of the map. In particular, review the legend, which explains what the various symbols represent and demonstrates what the markings for the various types of roads and trails on the map look like. Find the symbol for your intended hiking trail. It will usually be a line of dashes and may have a trail number badge on it.

On your map, find the trailhead you will be departing from. It will typically be indicated by a rounded black box with the initials TH on it. Next to it will be printed the name of the trail. As you scan up the trail route, you will often find a trapezoid-shaped box with the trail number in it. Know both the name and number of the trail you plan to hike. While signs along the trail often list both a trail name and number, sometimes only one or the other is listed.

Highlight Your Starting Point

Draw a circle around the trailhead with a highlighter marker. In the field, this will help you quickly zero in on your trip's starting point, a reference you will want to look at frequently. Also, on the border of the map, you will find the map scale. Here, lines demonstrate what both a mile and a kilometer look like on the map. It will usually note what one inch on the map equates to, for example: 1 map inch = 0.6 mile. This scale will vary depending on the type of map you are using. Pretrip, scan and print a copy of the section with your intended trail on it. Take the copy with you on your trip as a backup, should you lose your primary map, not an uncommon occurrence.

As you drive to the trailhead, notice the geography of the area you will be hiking. Are there named rivers or creeks, obvious peaks, power lines, radio towers, or other notable landmarks? All such features will help you form a mental map of your location. When you arrive at the trailhead, you know exactly where you are. Your goal will be to maintain that certainty as you leave the trailhead and progress on your hike.

Orient the Map

At the trailhead, orient the map. Open the map on which you have drawn your starting-point circle. Hold the map in front of you or lay it on the ground. Visualize yourself standing in the circle and rotate the map until significant features on the map match up with the actual features you can see. This is known as terrain association.

A more accurate method is to use your compass to align your map. Almost all maps are printed so the top of the map faces north. Place your compass on the map with the side of the baseplate parallel to the west edge of the map. Make sure the compass housing is pointing to the top or north edge of the map. Rotate the map with the compass on it, until the compass's floating magnetic needle points to the north on the compass housing. The map is now oriented so that the true north of the map points to the magnetic north.

Compasses are influenced by being near metal. Do not use your car hood to orient your map. Also be alert to any metal in your pockets, such as your keys or cell phone. Using the two

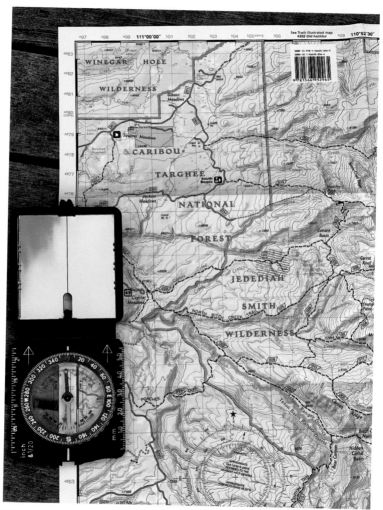

Allign your map to match the red north-pointing arrow on your compass.
Your map is now oriented.

Key Navigation Fundamentals

When learning backcountry map-and-compass navigation, here are some key concepts to understand:

True north. The geographic North Pole. Almost all maps are designed with the top of the map oriented to the true north.

Magnetic north. The point in the Arctic toward which magnetic compass needles point.

Magnetic declination. The difference between magnetic north and true north. It is expressed in degrees east or west of true north. You can buy a compass that can be adjusted to account for declination. The compass would then match the map, which uses true north.

Bearing. The compass direction from one spot to another, measured in degrees.

orientation methods of terrain association and map alignment together will yield a usable sense of the land around you.

Use the Map-Thumb Method

At the trailhead, note your starting altitude and the time you depart. If the trail is faint or you have chosen to travel cross-country, you may wish to use the map-thumb method. "Thumbing the map" means holding a folded map in your hand with the thumb on your present location. As you travel, you move your thumb along the route you are traveling. This allows you to note key landmarks without having to continuously find your location on the map.

For more established trails, you can track your progress by looking at the map at timed intervals (say every fifteen minutes) or as you encounter key landmarks (a bridge, a trail junction). When you review the map, compare the present time to your start time (be sure to check the time when you leave the trail-head), and you will have useful information by which to gauge your pace and estimate your travel speed.

Do a 180

One of the best navigation tips to avoid getting lost is to occasionally turn around 180 degrees and note what the trail looks like behind you. Things often look different upon your return, and this will establish some visual remembrances to help you confirm you are on the correct return path (assuming you are on an out-and-back trail, not a loop). This is especially important when undertaking early-morning alpine starts, when you are traveling in low light and focused on the goal of a distant summit.

Pay Attention to Signs

As you travel, take note of any directional trail signs you encounter. These often cite distances to key locations. A mile or two down the trail, it might be hard to recall any detail they included. If your memory is not perfect, take a photo of such signs to aid recall.

Triangulation

Triangulation is an excellent navigational tool to help you accurately locate where you are. It will work as long as you can identify two distinct landmarks that are at least 60 degrees apart. A landmark can be a mountain peak, a rock face, a lake, or a bridge—any prominent feature that appears on your map and you can see.

Once you've visually identified your landmarks, follow these steps:

1. Orient the map using your compass.
2. Find the two landmarks on your map.
3. Using your compass, take a bearing on each one by placing the compass on the map with one corner of the base plate on the landmark. Turn the compass on the map until the compass needle points north on the map. Draw a line on the map using the edge of the base plate. Repeat this process for the second landmark.
4. Your present location is approximately where the lines cross.

NAVIGATION MARKERS

Navigation markers are a series of small, man-made, physical signs strategically placed, usually at eye height, along a trail to assure you that you are following the correct trail. They are also commonly called confidence markers or trail markers. The US Forest Service trail-building publication calls them reassurance markers.

When you first begin hiking on a trail, you should look to see what type of markers were placed. Traditional markers were blazes cut in a tree with an ax, often in the shape of a lowercase letter *i*. Although still used, they are falling out of favor for environmental reasons.

Left: Painted-red metal marker   **Right:** Multicolor long-trail markers

Left: Square orange plastic marker **Right:** Blue diamond plastic marker

More common today are colored strips of metal or plastic nailed to a tree. These are usually sky blue, red, or yellow. On major long-distance trails, such as the Continental Divide Trail, you will find multicolor logos. You may also find trails marked with surveyors tape. This is usually done where trails have been recently rerouted. Be alert if you are following a specific color navigation marker and find that the markers change color. This may mean you are no longer on your planned trail.

In areas with few trees, markers may be placed on posts of cut lumber or narrow fiberglass posts. More commonly, you

Left: Branded post marker **Middle:** Blazed tree marker **Right:** Rock cairn marker

might find stone markers known as cairns. These stone towers are most often placed at trail junctions. Smaller rock markers of a few stones are known as ducks. Be wary of such rock piles because they may have been placed for reasons other than trail guidance. Marker use is dictated by various land management agencies. Be very alert in designated federal wilderness areas. In these areas, Leave No Trace principles often result in very few markers, if any at all. Those that exist may simply be unmarked fence posts.

The Most Likely Places to Lose Your Way

Blowdowns. Blowdowns are jumbles of uprooted trees that are caused by severe windstorms or microbursts. It can take overworked trail crews years to clear them from hiking trails. Blowdowns force you off the original route and onto a maze of newly created social trails. This is a good place to flag your route or to use compass bearings to circumvent the entire mess.

Summits. As you approach a hard-earned summit above tree line, your focus is on the prize and not on your ascent route. You can get turned around on a rounded, rock-strewn, or snowcapped summit as you take photos, snack, and relax. It is easy to lose track of which ridgeline you ascended. It is wise to mark your return direction before you rest. A simple and effective way to mark the ridge is by laying your hiking poles pointing in the correct direction.

Trail Intersections. When you approach a Y intersection on a trail, the correct choice of travel may be obvious. This is not always the case when you are returning. Mark the correct choice with sticks, rocks, or flagging tape (but don't forget to remove it later!) so it is apparent upon your return.

Transitions. Any kind of a topography transition can be confusing upon your return. A classic is a trail that progresses through a forest, then spills you out into a large meadow. Upon return, such locations can be hard to spot in the forest edge and should be marked.

Cutting Switchbacks. This practice is bad for the environment and can be bad for you as well if the trail does not take the turn you expected and for which you thought you were headed. The US Forest Service guidelines for trail builders encourages that switchbacks be constructed with a steeper grade than the rest of the trail to discourage trail cutting. This construction practice makes cutting switchbacks more likely to add to one's confusion and enhances the likelihood of losing the trail. Also be careful to avoid walking straight off the end of a switchback. Water-diversion structures or erosion from water runoff there can mimic a trail.

Bathroom Breaks. Stepping off the trail into a forest for a bathroom break can be disorienting. Your goal is to seek privacy and be hidden from the trail, which puts you at risk of losing the trail. If in a group, let someone know what you are doing. Always take your pack with you, just in case you cannot find your way back and must survive.

Separating from Your Group or Partner. A group that splits up is a classic cause of lost hikers. Research shows that groups make better decisions than individuals. They possess a larger amount of information and equipment than solitary individuals. Survival chances are better with larger numbers. When a lone hiker must make a route decision, they consider the information available and proceed on the course they select. Groups have checking mechanisms. One member can raise questions about a decision choice, and a wiser decision may result.

THE STORY CONTINUES . . .

Despite these many helpful tips, in our introductory story I am still lost. Let's see how I handle the situation in the coming chapter, which lays out tips for surviving being lost.

10

Lost

DON'T LET THIS HAPPEN TO YOU

In our story, I have gone far enough off the trail that when I turn around to look for it, it cannot be seen. Dread, terror, bewilderment, confusion, unsettledness, and panic set in.

THE ABOVE LIST includes words researchers have used to describe a lost hiker's response to an intense psychological condition known as woods shock. It commonly occurs when you first notice you are no longer on the trail you have been following. You want this unpleasantness to end, and in response, you may randomly charge into the woods, seeking recognizable territory. If it doesn't appear soon, a typical next step is to speed up your search, perhaps running frantically through the forest. By this point, you are frightened, embarrassed, maybe even panic-stricken. You might think, *I am an experienced outdoorsperson. This can't have* *happened to me!* Those who have encountered woods shock report that years later, recalling the incident, their blood pressure rises, muscles tense, and palms sweat.

MANAGING THE SITUATION

The psychological emotions that accompany being lost may make you feel incompetent, weak, or lacking in courage. But increasingly, science disagrees. Neurologists now believe that the emotions you feel are based in primitive survival mechanisms. We all create mental maps of our home, neighborhood, and community. The frantic running and scrambling are efforts to reconnect with the larger territorial area we all must navigate to survive. The frenetic activity is set off by adrenaline, cortisol, and other stress hormones flooding the body. Emerging data indicates that the amino acid glutamate is a key neurotransmitter in lost-person behavior.

So how do you harness that and make your best next move? There are steps you can take to manage the situation.

1. STOP and Assess

When you recognize you are lost and you feel panic begin to grip you, do all you can to assess the current situation. First, mark the spot where you initially recognized you were lost. Ideally, you will reach into your pack for surveyors tape and carefully mark the location. It may be difficult to do this calmly when fighting increasing panic. Methodical searching through your pack while anxiety accelerates may be too much to overcome. At the very least, before you move, mark the spot with a small cairn of rocks or sticks stacked as a tepee. If that still feels like too much, grab tissue or TP from your pack and throw it to the ground. Congratulations! You have just secured a critical geographical landmark that can be the key to becoming unlost. We call this the first lost point (FLP), and it will serve as an important clue to getting back on track. If you could fly a drone high over the forest, you would see there is a direct line from the FLP back to the missing trail.

A "first lost point" (FLP) marker

The FLP will be further explored when we discuss techniques for getting unlost.

Do all you can to fight the pressing need to scramble away. **Sit or kneel near your FLP.** Your aim is to stop reacting and start thinking as clearly as you can. Think of the anagram STOP: Sit. Think. Observe. Plan. Attempt to calm yourself and move from reaction to proactivity. Let's look at each in more detail.

Sit. Rest and recover from the shock of becoming lost. Drink water and have a snack as you decide what to do next.

Think. Analyze where you are and how or where you might have gotten off track. Which way is north? Where was the last place you were clearly on the trail? What time of day was it? Who

Everyday Items That Can Be Used for Survival

If in backcountry trouble, it is ideal to have the Ten Essentials. But develop resourceful thinking and you will always have more survival items than you think. You likely have numerous safety items close at hand.

Water Bottle. When held in sunlight, a full water bottle can create a focused spot of sun, which, when directed on balled-up dry leaves, can start a campfire.

Wallet. Your wallet likely contains a credit card or driver's license with a hologram security seal that can work as a highly reflective surface for signaling. Paper money can serve as kindling or be rolled into a sipping straw to drink from shallow seeps.

Comb. A comb is easy to light and will burn hot for a long time. It is useful as a fire starter with wet wood. Lint from your pockets also works well.

Socks. Use socks as mittens when you get cold, as your feet will retain some heat from your shoes. Pants pockets can also be removed and used as mittens.

Shirt. To obtain bandage material, rip off the lower two inches of your T-shirt.

Ballpoint Pen. A plastic pen with its ballpoint cartridge removed can be a straw for sipping water from shallow puddles or from between rocks.

Key. A key can become a cutting blade by scraping it on concrete or a rock. A flashlight or small pocketknife may be carried on your key chain.

Belt. Elastic or web belts can become emergency tourniquets.

Cell Phone. Your phone likely contains a flashlight and has GPS capability. A broken screen can be used as a knife. A piece of wire held to both ends of a salvaged cell phone battery will get red hot at the center. Apply this to a tinder bundle and blow to start a fire.

Eyeglasses. The clear-glass lens of spectacles can serve as a fire starter. In sunlight, focus the sun's rays on a bundle of easily ignited material, such as tissue, toilet paper, or pocket lint. Have a tinder bundle and kindling readily available.

did you leave your travel plans with, and when would they report you missing?

Inventory your resources. This can be a very comforting step to take. If you have the Ten Essentials, remind yourself that you are well equipped to survive. If you have less gear, you still likely have more resources than you think. And remember, everyday items can be turned into survival gear.

Observe. Are there people around? Can you see or hear them? Are there major landmarks nearby or lifelines that lead to people, such as powerlines or rivers? What is the weather doing? Should a shelter be built? Are there hills nearby to improve phone reception or for observation and signaling purposes?

Plan. Can you self-rescue, and find the lost trail using wagon-wheel techniques (see page 160)? Do you have time to search before nightfall?

Set priorities for action. Priorities always start with treating any life-threatening injuries. If you have an injured hiking partner, follow the ABCDE's, as taught in Wilderness First Aid. Here is a brief rundown:

- **A:** Make sure the person's **airway** is clear. If not, adjust the head and clear the throat. Remove anything impeding air, such as gum, dentures, or food.
- **B:** Is the person **breathing**?
- **C:** Is there **circulation**? Does the person have a pulse? If not, start CPR. Is the person bleeding? If so, can it be stopped? Elevate and apply pressure to wounds.
- **D** for **disability**: Is there harm to the neck or spine? If so, immobilize the person.
- **E** for **environment**: Is the person exposed to the weather or cold ground? Place insulation under the person and dress them warmly.

Address additional priorities, sometimes called "the rule of three," in this order:

1. **Shelter.** In foul weather, you cannot survive much beyond three hours without finding or creating a shelter.
2. **Water.** One is unlikely to live beyond three days without water.
3. **Food.** Three weeks is usually how long one can survive without food.

2. Take Action

You have calmly considered your circumstances and set your priorities. While remaining near the point where you noticed that you were first lost (FLP), try yelling for help. If you are separated from a group or a camp, they may be nearer than you think. If you have a whistle, blow it. A whistle can be heard at a much longer distance than a human voice. Three blasts of a whistle are a call for help. (See proper whistle protocol in Appendix C.)

If daylight remains, attempt to find your lost path. Near the FLP, create the most visible base marker you can. Use surveyors flagging tape, bright clothing, or other highly visible items. Except in winter, white is a rare color in nature. A white T-shirt or toilet paper clearly stands out in a green forest, red sandstone desert, or sagebrush meadow.

If you have left details of your itinerary with a trustworthy individual and can expect searchers, it is best to remain near the FLP. Searchers are likely to travel your intended route, and the FLP is probably near it. If you leave the site to search for the trail, climb to a view spot, or look for water, always return to near the FLP.

There are a few techniques you might adopt at this stage: the wagon-wheel technique or the compass-point technique.

Wagon-Wheel Technique

From your FLP and visible marker, walk toward what you suspect is the most likely direction of your lost trail. Try to follow a straight line. Count the number of paces as you walk, going no more than 100 or so paces. One pace is counted as each time you use the same foot—*left, right, left, right* equals two paces. Keep the marker you created in sight. Only travel out of sight of the base marker if you mark your path with stakes, stone cairns, or broken branches so you can readily return to your starting-point base marker.

If your first effort is unsuccessful, try again, walking in another direction about 20 degrees away from your first effort. Envision a wagon wheel or bicycle wheel, with your starting marker as the hub and each effort as a spoke. Continue traveling various spokes until you encounter the lost trail.

Compass-Point Technique

The compass-point technique is similar to the wagon wheel technique, but here, you follow the major points of the compass, (N, NE, E, SE, S, SW, W, NW) while you search for the trail. In this method, you hold your compass as you walk the spokes of the compass. The method can be more precise than the wagon wheel and can work better in areas with low visibility, such as forests or willow fields.

WAITING FOR RESCUE

While waiting for rescue at or near your FLP, attempt to make your presence as visible as possible. Display any bright-colored clothing or tent material you have. If it can be done safely, build a fire. During daylight, make the fire smoky by burning green foliage. At night, build the fire high and bright. The ideal emergency fire signal consists of three separate fires placed in a triangle pattern, 50 feet apart.

If aircraft appear, signal to them with a mirror. Hold one arm straight out toward the aircraft and sight along it toward your hand. Hold the mirror near your face and flash the sun's reflection at your extended hand, making a "V" sign with two fingers, with the aircraft target beyond it.

If you do not have a mirror, you can use a credit card hologram, the silver base of a propane cannister, the silver interior wrapper of an energy bar, the base of an aluminum soda can polished with toothpaste to make it shine, or the glass face of a cell phone.

Ground-to-Air Signals

Know the recognized ground signals, as featured here. If you can only remember a few, create an X or V. Straight lines are

Aircraft ground rescue signals. Illustration by Margaret DeLuca

uncommon in nature and will stand out. If your FLP site is in a forest, create a large arrow pointing to it from a nearby open space.

Search pilots, such as Civil Air Patrol, are trained to recognize ground signals. Signals should be at least 30 feet long. You can form them using lines of brush, tree branches, or rocks. In an open snow-covered field, stamp out your message. SOS is a universally recognized message. In the United States, the word HELP is well understood.

STEPS SEARCHERS WILL TAKE

When notified, SAR authorities will attempt to gather as much information as possible from the reporter—the trusted individual with whom you left your Leave a Trace trip plan. It is likely the

Civil Air Patrol preps for a mission. Photo by Sanjay Tyagi

reporter may receive contacts from several agencies and may be repeatedly asked the same questions. Reporters should stay close to their phones. The well-respected SAR guide *Lost Person Behavior* lists twenty-six questions responders should ask reporters about the lost hikers. These include, but are not limited to:

▸ Years of experience at hiking? Frequency?
▸ Years of experience in the area? Frequency?
▸ Purpose of hike—any goals? For example, photography, exercise?
▸ Navigational ability? Competent with map and compass?
▸ Able to hike at night? Off trail?
▸ Planning for this hike or typical planning habits for similar hikes?

▸ Have you checked the lost person's computer browsing history for weather forecasts, alternate location/destination?
▸ Pictures available of past hikes showing their equipment?

They will summon SAR volunteers or coordinate with employed staff, such as sheriff deputies, rangers, Civil Air Patrol spotters, and fire departments. This activity takes time, and when reports are made late in the day, searching may not occur until the following day. For safety reasons, searchers sometimes do not search at night. Exceptions are often made for children and people with dementia. Those lost should expect to spend at least one night out.

SAR leadership typically establishes an incident command post (ICP). Searchers are usually directed to a last known point (LKP). This is a spot at which a major clue, such as parked car or known used trailhead, is correlated to the missing person. Another key location is where the search subject was last observed, often referred to as PLS, or place last seen.

Searchers often first dispatch a small, lightly equipped immediate response team, called a hasty team. They will attempt to quickly find and stabilize the individual, assess the hiker's condition, and provide further direction to SAR leadership regarding the hiker's needs.

BUILDING A SHELTER

If forced to spend a night out, begin two hours before sunset to build a shelter. In the Rocky Mountain West, expect the nights to be very cool. If safe to do so, build a fire for warmth, for comfort, and to assist in being found. Your shelter should be near the fire, but at least 6 feet away and between the fire and the prevailing wind. Cold settles at night, so avoid locations near streambeds and rivers. Higher locations are warmer, as are forested areas. In mountainous areas, get below timberline. Select a well-drained location where water will not settle after a rainstorm.

If you have a tarp, pitch it as a lean-to, facing the fire. Do all you can to insulate yourself from the ground. Pine branches are

Survive the night. Dig in under a debris pile.

easy to break off even if you have no tools. Stack pine branches at least 3 feet deep on the ground where you will be lying down. Gather an equal amount to place over you. This is called a debris pile.

Lacking a tarp, create a debris hut. Build it by leaning a central wooden ridge pole against a tree, large rock, or a bipod of logs. Use two angled poles to frame an opening at the highest spot and place branches on both sides in descending length until they reach where the ridge pole touches the ground. Then place pine boughs, brush, moss, tree bark, leaves, or sagebrush over the branch framework.

Ideally, the outer layer will be dense enough to stop breezes and rainfall. Place additional pine boughs or dried leaves or grass inside the shelter for insulation. Keep the shelter small and low, with just enough room to lie in and to minimize air space. The less air space, the more easily it will be heated by your body.

At night, sleep with a hat or neck gaiter covering your head. Check your backpack for an internal back pad. Most of these can be removed. Lie on it and place your feet inside your pack. If your boots are dry, sleep with them on but loosen the laces to increase warmth from circulation. In the cold, sleep with all your warm layers on. Even wrap-around sunglasses and layers of sunscreen will help retain warmth.

When you leave your camp to gather materials, always carry minimal essentials, such as your headlamp, an extra layer, and a knife. Pay attention to your route back to camp.

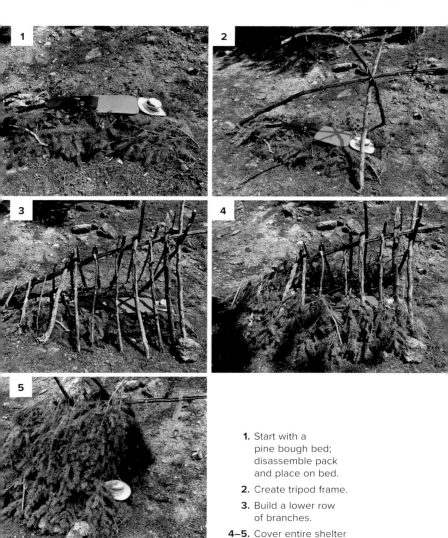

1. Start with a pine bough bed; disassemble pack and place on bed.
2. Create tripod frame.
3. Build a lower row of branches.
4–5. Cover entire shelter with branches.

Drink plenty of water. It may seem counterintuitive on cold nights, but the body's heating system works best when well hydrated.

THE REST OF THE STORY . . .

I turn around 180 degrees. No sign of the trail. I walk about 30 feet back the way I knew I came. Still no trail. This is scary, and I might be "officially" lost, *I think to myself.* Now, what was the first thing I was supposed to do? Ah right, mark the spot. *I head back to where the realization first hit me, my FLP. I take a bandana from my pocket and throw it down. Not as fancy as surveyors tape, but it will suffice.*

Now what? A deep breath. I sit down, drink some water, and try to remember the last place I was unlost. OK, it's still early in the day. I am well equipped, with my Ten Essentials and plenty of snacks and water.

I decide to set up a wagon wheel. First, I build a better, more visible FLP base marker. I dig out the flagging tape, and on it, I write my name, the time and date, and that I am lost. Then, I build a sturdy, high, tepee-type construction to hang it on.

With my compass, I take a bearing on the way I think I first came from. I start walking down the line, trying to stay as straight on the bearing as I can. Also, I look back frequently to make sure I can still see the base marker. And then, I get very lucky. Two hundred feet down the line, I find the trail!

Forest Fires

The view of the Teton Range in northwestern Wyoming is spectacular. It becomes even more compelling as you approach the base of these famous peaks. Our remote, permit-only wilderness campsite was about as close as we could get and still find level ground to pitch a tent. Adding to our already remarkable view was a display of nature unlike anything either my wife or I had ever seen. Major late-summer forest fires were occurring 20 miles to the west in neighboring Idaho. High easterly winds sent deep-purple smoke clouds billowing over the Teton Range in a truly remarkable spectacle. The evening's low light highlighted the fast-moving clouds with bright-orange accents and golden flashes wherever the sun broke through.

We left our campsite to better watch this colorful light show, hiking a half mile to a rocky peninsula jutting into the nearby mountain lake. We watched spellbound until evening darkness

Forest fire in Grand Teton National Park

started to close in. We turned east and started back to our campsite. It was then we noticed that Wyoming and Grand Teton National Park had developed its own raging wildfire. It was spreading rapidly and was directly beyond our campsite, over a small ridge. Our access trail was now buried under dense smoke, and exit by the trail we hiked in on was completely cut off.

FOREST FIRES are a valid concern for backcountry travelers. Forest Service officials report an increasing severity of fires and growing damage to public lands and neighboring communities.

For example, the average length of fire season in the Western US is now seventy days longer than it was just one generation ago. Forests are challenged by weather changes, beetle kill, and urban growth and development.

While it's useful to understand overarching trends, they are simply background information. The most important sources of immediate danger are entities that are much harder to predict: people. Human carelessness accounts for nearly nine out of ten wildfires. We smoke on forest trails, allow campfires and slash piles to escape, park overheated cars in roadside weeds, and light firecrackers. Indeed, the Fourth of July routinely sets the annual record for the most new fires. In North America, people accidently cause over 62,000 fires per year. Although nature does its part as well, it runs a distant second, with lightning identified as the source of an average of 10,000 fires per year. Forest fire growth has led to what the Department of Agriculture describes as skyrocketing fire-fighting costs.

As those who care about the great outdoors and are major beneficiaries of public land recreation, we must practice responsible backcountry fire safety. We need to do so not only to keep others and ourselves out of danger, but also to preserve forests and wildlife for future generations.

ASSESSING FIRE DANGER, FIRE RESTRICTIONS, AND CLOSURES

The Rocky Mountain region is unique, with huge areas of public lands administered by numerous governmental agencies. This includes national parks, national forests, Bureau of Land

Barometer fire-danger sign

Management (BLM) lands, state parks, state and federal wildlife areas, regional parks, county parks, and city-owned mountain parks. Standards and regulations differ from agency to agency, so it is important to know who administers the area in which you plan to hike, particularly in fire season. Check with them prior to your visit. These entities usually have websites or phone numbers you can use to contact them and learn of any restrictions in place. Perhaps the simplest way to determine who has jurisdiction of your planned hiking route is to consult the Trails Illustrated Maps published by National Geographic. These maps highlight the different jurisdictions by color, making land management agencies easy to identify.

While there may be as many fire regulations as there are governing entities, they can generally be classified in either of two major categories: daily fire danger warnings or mandatory bans.

▸ **Daily fire danger warnings** are often posted along roadways by fire districts and national forest land managers. These signs indicate danger with a standard barometer of green, blue, yellow, orange, or red colors. They also have standardized levels of fire danger, from low through moderate, high, very high, and extreme. Hikers should routinely check these signs when heading into rural areas.

▸ A second level of restrictions concern **mandatory burn bans** established by regional fire or law enforcement authorities. In Colorado, for example, county sheriff departments have statutory authority to impose mandatory fire restrictions. These only occur during periods of extreme fire danger and should be carefully observed. These are designated as stage 1, 2, and 3, with 3 being the most restrictive. Additional prohibited activities accompany each level. **Stage 1** bans occur frequently in summer months but can be imposed year-round. Typically, this level of ban prohibits the use of campfires, stoves, and grills of any kind. Included in the ban are fires in stone rings in dispersed campsites, as well as alcohol, twig, and solid-fuel stoves. Exceptions are firepits and pedestal grills at developed campsites and pressurized backpacking stoves with on-off controls. **Stage 2** bans include prohibition of most types of backpacking stoves, including white gas and solid-fuel stoves. Only pressurized canister stoves are permitted. **Stage 3** bans prohibit all camping activity and all stove use, including pressurized canister stoves.

Fire restriction levels are generally similar across jurisdictions. However, individual entities often include subtle variations in postings. Therefore, it is wise to specifically review each organization's posting. Although the varying restrictions

may be confusing at first, they are an essential part of trip planning: If you're on a public trail, you're responsible for understanding current conditions. Violations of these regulations are a Class B misdemeanor, punishable by fines of not more than $5,000 for individuals or $10,000 for an organization or imprisonment for not more than six months, or both.

Fire ban signs

BACKCOUNTRY FIRE SAFETY

When you enter the backcountry, pay attention to any smoke you detect. See if you can locate its source and determine if it's under control. Be particularly concerned if you know a fire ban is in effect and you smell smoke.

Study the smoke. Smoke scattered across an entire valley and moving in one direction suggests a fire will spread rapidly and tells you where the fire will go. A safer situation is if you see smoke rising vertically into the sky, indicating minimal wind conditions. If, at night, you spot a red glow in the atmosphere, a fire may be in your area.

As you hike through an area in fire season, observe the condition of the trail or escape routes that may slow you down if you need to evacuate. Note the location of natural features, such as rocky patches, water, and meadows. Be situationally aware and watch for safe zones, such as clear-cuts, roads, trails, and helicopter landing spots.

Escape Routes and Safety Zones

Weather and terrain both have an effect on mountain wildfires. Temperatures, wind speed, relative humidity, and precipitation all combine to shape the speed and intensity of wildfires. Topography dramatically influences fire direction. Fires will burn more rapidly uphill. A box canyon can create a chimney effect, which will draw a fire rapidly up a canyon. Fire on one side of a narrow canyon can quickly jump across to the other side. Sparks and embers can be spread up to three-quarters of a mile by wind gusts.

Fires tend to start in dry, dead vegetation. Green, moist plants have some protection, but this is lost when fire heat builds and dries out surrounding vegetation, in a process known as preheating. This, in turn, causes higher intensity and faster-moving fire behavior.

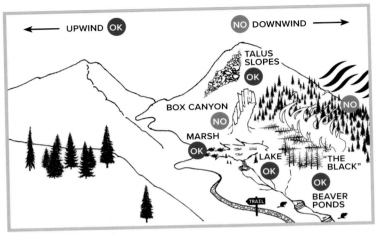

Look for safety zones in case of a wildfire. Illustration by Margaret DeLuca

Do not underestimate fire behavior. Never try to outrun a fire. They can travel up to 20 miles an hour. Do not choose escape routes that are steep and uphill. Avoid locations that are upslope or downwind from a fire. Chimneys, saddles, and narrow canyons are dangerous areas to pass through.

Observe the direction of the fire and attempt to be on its flank, or better yet, get behind it. Blackened, burned-over areas are safer than untouched locations. "Get in the black" is a classic admonition from firefighters. Fires attract observers, including airplanes, helicopters, and drones. Make yourself visible by carrying a bright-colored tarp or tent fly.

If you have done your best to avoid a fire, but now find you must escape it, mark the location of flames on your map. Look for safe locations on the map that take you away from the fire and toward emergency services. This could be trailheads, roads, local neighborhoods, mine locations, or established fire breaks. Orient your map—turn it so the top of the map page is to the north as indicated by your compass. Determine a compass bearing from your location to the safe spot you identified. A bearing will be helpful if smoke becomes too heavy to easily see through. Follow the bearing to safety.

In the worst-case situation of being surrounded by fire, you must seek a refuge location and go to ground. This can be rocky slopes or areas above tree line where there is less fuel. Beaver ponds, lakes, and creeks can offer safety, although they pose hypothermia risks. In a last resort, find the nearest, least vegetated area, ideally, a moist low spot. Lie facedown, with your feet toward the fire. Heat rises, so stay as low as you can. If you can dig lower or cover yourself with dirt, do so. You can also dig a small hole, cup your hands around your face, and breathe through it. Stay put and hope the fire quickly passes over your location.

Hiking in Fire-Burned Areas

Charred forests are dangerous for years after a fire. Avoid them if you can. If you cannot, travel through them quickly. Whole trees or damaged limbs can drop without warning. Do not sit or camp under these trees, especially on windy days.

Root systems that have burnt out provide invisible, underground sink holes to trap an ankle or foot. Trails become hard to locate. Signs and route markers may have vanished, making

Blackened, already burned-over areas are safer to be in than unburned areas during a wildfire.

navigation difficult. After fires, trails are prone to rolling rocks and mudslides. There will likely be numerous logs across the trail. Burned trees are much more likely to topple, making a trail hard to follow. The newly exposed ground holds less water, and snow melts more rapidly. Streams can flood to dangerous levels, blocking stream crossings.

After a fire, land managers may officially close an area for months or even years. Stay out of these areas. In the event you harm yourself in these unstable areas, you run the risk of putting search and rescue workers in danger, as well, if there is a need for you to be rescued.

Campfires are the largest man-made cause of wildfires.

Risks of Battling a Fire

If a fire starts near you, you may be able to battle it in its early stages. Remove fuel sources, such as branches, and throw water and dirt on it. Do not fight a fire if it endangers you or your group. Fires can cause dangerous injuries, such as burns, which require immediate first aid or medical attention. In addition, super-heated air can cause burns without flames touching the body. If inhaled, this air can damage and burn lung tissue. Fire-generated carbon monoxide can cause rapid asphyxiation. Remove the victim from the smoky location and seek treatment for carbon monoxide poisoning. Provide oxygen if available. Under both conditions, rapid evacuation, medical evaluation, and a blood test are imperative.

CAMPFIRES

Campfires are a classic backcountry experience. However, their use is declining as their negative impact on the environment becomes better understood. Campfires sterilize the ground around them, and they are the leading cause of forest fires. Many experienced hikers and backpackers go years without building a fire. However, the focus of this book is safety, and there are legitimate times when building a fire can prove lifesaving.

When weather conditions border on causing hypothermia, fires will provide a much-needed heat source. They rapidly dry wet clothing and sterilize drinking water. If a stove fails, they allow for the preparation of hot food, which can revive exhausted campers. In emergency and accident situations, campfires revitalize sagging emotions and add comfort. This is helpful for lost individuals. Smoking fires can serve as a signal to searchers.

If circumstances call for building a fire, seek an already disturbed area or existing fire ring. A large fire is rarely necessary. If possible, it is best to build the fire near a water source. If available, use only dead and down wood—do not break branches from trees, even ones that appear to be dead. Do not leave your fire unattended.

When the fire is no longer needed, drown the fire site with a mixture of water and dirt. To make sure you have extinguished all burning material, move hot sticks and branches around. Continue adding water and stirring until you can detect no heat from the embers on the back of your ungloved hand.

A hidden danger exists when a campfire comes in contact with forest duff, deteriorating organic matter that may look like soil. Duff can smolder underground for days and can reignite a fire long after you have left it.

What to Wear to a Fire

It's unlikely you will have an extensive wardrobe selection in an emergency fire situation. But there are a few things to consider if you have the time and the options.

Although synthetics are recommended for almost all outdoor situations, avoid them in forest fires. They tend to melt and can cause severe skin burns. Historically, wool is a firefighter's choice. Shed your nylon hiking pants and escape the fire in your long, merino-wool base layers. Wear the brightest clothes you have. Airplanes are more likely to spot you through the smoke.

When I was first caught in a forest fire in my neighborhood woods at age 8, I developed a plan that, in my next escape, I would soak my clothes in a stream and run through the flames. Luckily, age brings wisdom, and I learned that this was a terrible plan. Make your escape in dry clothes, if at all possible. Wet clothing turns scorching hot in the radiated heat of a fire. This is similar to the effect you see in blue jeans when you iron them with a steam iron. The same goes for a water-soaked bandana across your face: Don't do it. You will scorch your lips and lungs.

REPORTING A FIRE

When you escape a fire, do not simply go home. Always report your location and experience to fire authorities as quickly as possible once you are out of danger. This can save lives and property. Cars at the trailhead may be burnt and trail registers destroyed. You want to avoid the risk to rescuers who may think you are still in danger.

By reporting the fire to authorities, many lives may be saved through immediate intervention. When you report a fire, expect to be asked for the following information:

- ▸ The location, map reference, nearest trail, drainage, or mountain name
- ▸ The best-known access point and estimated miles and time to reach the fire
- ▸ A timeline of the events you experienced
- ▸ An estimate of the fire size
- ▸ Color of the smoke column
- ▸ If you saw flames and, if so, how long ago
- ▸ The types of fuels that were burning
- ▸ A description of the weather
- ▸ If there were thunderstorms or lightning
- ▸ If there were other people in the area and if you spoke to them. Try to note a description of individuals, numbers, hair color, clothing, and other identifying details. This is important for their safety, as well as for the fire investigation.

A young wildfire building

THE REST OF THE STORY . . .

It was too late in the evening to consider a cross-country escape. We moved our tent as close to the mountain lake as we were able. We packed our backpacks and climbed into our sleeping bags fully clothed. Our nervous planning included the idea of launching into the lake with our blow-up air mattresses.

Sleep did not come easily that night and was interrupted by a loud clapping sound, emanating from the deep forest behind us. Our late-night visitor was a National Park ranger, who had traveled cross-country through grizzly territory to warn us of the forest fire. Because of the park's permit system, the ranger knew exactly where we were camped that night. The clapping was the ranger's way of alerting the bears to a human presence in the night.

Our hero gave us orders not to leave our campsite without National Park direction. We were safer by the lake than wandering on fire-engulfed trails. The rangers knew where we were and wanted us to stay so they could come directly to us should we need rescue. The ranger then set off, using compass bearings, heading for the next group of campers.

The next day, we returned to our viewpoint on the lake. This time, the spectacular scenery was all man-made. For hours, we watched as bucket-carrying helicopters swooped low over the lake and scooped up water to dump on the nearby fire. We came to recognize the various aircraft and individual pilots.

On the third day of the fire, we were free to leave. While driving out of the fire area, we ran into a ranger manning a barrier across the road. Nearby, a map display had been set up to educate park visitors about the fire. The ranger told us they suspected visitors climbing and camping in a nearby bouldering area had caused the fire. He was glad to see we had gotten out safely. As were we.

12

Animal Encounters

When I encountered the bears, they were about 50 feet away. A mother and her cub had their heads down, rooting for necessary calories. The cub saw me first and ran away to my left at full speed. I yelled, "Hey Bear," and tried to look big and intimidating. The mother bear jerked her head up, startled, and ran off to my right. Wow, *I thought,* what just happened? *I took a deep breath and began to process the event. I decided it was another case of black bears being very timid around humans. I'd run into bears a dozen times, and each time they bolted away, not to be seen again. Except this time . . . Mom had apparently realized her cub was missing and likely assumed I had something to do with it. She crashed out of the forest and was charging directly toward me like a speeding locomotive.*

SEEING WILD ANIMALS in the backcountry is one of the joys of wilderness travel. It is a glorious and humbling experience to encounter the royalty of the forest and healthy to contemplate that humans are not always at the top of the food chain. We are visitors in their backyards. It is a privilege to view them, and it is our responsibility to disturb them as little as possible. If our actions cause them to change their behavior, we have gotten too close.

There are over 300 species of mammals in the Rocky Mountains. We can consider ourselves fortunate to see even a few. Most have learned to fear people and willingly flee from encounters. The few who do not are ones to be concerned about from a personal safety point of view.

National Park Service naturalists warn that all wildlife can be dangerous. They recommend staying at least 25 yards from moose, bison, and elk. When observing bears and wolves, stay a minimum of 100 yards away.

More often than you might think, people have attempted to raise wild animals as pets. Animals accustomed to humans can be especially dangerous. There are many ways they may have learned that humans are a source of food. Others may have a disease, such as rabies, which can cause them to lose their fear. Be on guard when any wild animal approaches you; it is almost never for a positive purpose. Also be alert around any newborn or young animals. A protective parent is almost certainly nearby. Do not approach or touch any infant animals. And do not feed any animal (not even a chipmunk), despite how cute and hungry they appear. Never, ever get between a mother animal and her offspring.

In the wilderness, it is best to avoid wearing perfumes and scents, as they can attract curious predators. Pick up and pack out all food scraps and food wrappers. Do not bury garbage near campsites or leave foil or tin cans in campfire rings or campsite area. You may have avoided an unwanted animal visit, but your carelessness can cause problems for the next hiker who uses your campsite.

MOUNTAIN LIONS

Mountain lions, also known as cougars, catamounts, pumas, or panthers, are magnificent, graceful animals. They are the largest cat in North America, weighing an average of 150 pounds and are up to eight feet in length. Territorial, with ranges varying in area from 10 to 370 square miles, they mark their boundaries with piles of twigs, forest litter, feces, urine, and dirt. Deer is their preferred food source, but they also eat birds, porcupines, and elk. They will hunt household pets, particularly as the cougars age and lose the ability to capture wild game. Lions are stealthy and travel silently. They will stalk their game and attack it from behind, seeking to break the victim's neck with a bite from their powerful jaws.

In the Western United States, it is very likely you have hiked through mountain lion territory. While it is rare to see one, you can be sure they have seen you. Studies using radio-collared lions track them stealthily lingering in mountain neighborhoods, watching domestic animals, and settling down near school playgrounds.

Contact with humans has increased as we move into their traditional territories. Although increasing, attacks on adult humans remain very rare. Children may be more of a target, as their high voices, small sizes, and busy movements more closely emulate smaller prey.

Best practices when hiking in lion country:

▸ Ideally, hike in groups of two or more. If hiking solo, use trekking poles, which add to your noise and help keep you from surprising lions.
▸ Do not wear earbuds, which limit hearing and situational awareness.
▸ Watch for lion tracks, which appear like large housecat tracks.
▸ Watch for stick and pine needle mounds, which lions create to hide fresh kills. They often return to these sites. If you discover one, leave the area immediately.
▸ If you encounter a lion, do not imitate prey:
    • Stand tall, making yourself look as big as possible. Hold open your jacket and lift it behind your head.
    • Neither run nor stand still. Back away slowly, looking the lion in the eye and speaking firmly and loudly.
    • Bending over can make you look like four-legged prey. But if possible, grab rocks or branches to throw at the lion.
    • Throw your backpack at the lion.

Mountain lion

- If you have children, pick them up. Do not let them run. If they are older, stand in front of them.
- If a lion attacks, fight back. If knocked down, get up, make loud noises, use anything within reach to fight the lion.
- If you have an air horn or bear spray, use it on the lion.

MOOSE

Moose, common in the American West, are found mainly in Idaho, Montana, Colorado, Wyoming, and eastern Utah. They are less abundant in Washington and Oregon. Rare sightings occur in California and New Mexico. They are iconic and charismatic animals. In nature, they have few enemies and thus are often approachable. However, they are very territorial and getting too close can be a serious mistake. The Colorado Department of Parks and Wildlife has declared them the most dangerous animal in Colorado.

Moose are often encountered in riparian areas that are lush with willows and abundant brush. They do not form herds, as do elk and deer. They are most often found alone or in small groups, typically a mother and her young. While it is possible to get fairly close to moose, they seem to have a clear limit as to how much of their space they will allow you to invade. You are much too close if they raise the long hairs on their hump, lay back their ears, and lick their snout. If you observe any of these signs, you are in grave danger. Back away immediately, but do not run.

Moose

Moose can travel quickly and can attack with antlers or hooves. If charged by a moose, try to get behind a tree or large rock.

Dogs and moose do not mix. Moose see canines as if they are wolves, a historic enemy. An unleashed dog may approach a moose and incite a charge. Dogs will often then escape back to their owner, bringing along the angry moose.

BEARS

Bears are iconic symbols of American forests. They show up in childhood fairy tales, popular cartoons, and local news reports, and are the subject of the most common questions in hiking safety classes. These large, adaptive animals have survived the encroachment of man and are thriving throughout much of the American West, from deep wilderness to forested and urban areas. Should you encounter one, how you behave is dictated by the type of bear.

Black Bears

Don't let the name fool you. The North American black bear comes in many colors, from jet black to brown, cinnamon, blond, and red. Males can weigh over 400 pounds. The largest on record weighed 805 pounds. They are powerful and athletic. They can easily outrun a man and have been clocked at more than 25 miles per hour. They are omnivores and will eat anything they consider edible, though most of their diet is vegetable matter. They also eat decaying carcasses, insects, fish, small animals, and human garbage.

Black bear

Brown Bears

Brown bears are the largest apex predator in North America, mostly found in coastal Alaska and Canada. Grizzly bears are a slightly smaller, inland form. They are rare, except around Yellowstone National Park, Glacier National Park, and increasingly, Grand Teton National Park. There are also a few in the North Cascade mountains of Washington. Once close to extinction in the lower forty-eight states, their populations are slowly expanding, due to recovery-management efforts. Grizzlies no longer live in Colorado. The last one was killed in 1979 by a bow hunter in the San Juan Mountains.

Grizzly and brown bears can be blond, black, or brown. They have a distinct shoulder hump and short, rounded ears, and their face has a dished profile. They have good eyesight and an extraordinary sense of smell.

All bears are most active in the cool of the morning and early evenings. During the heat of the day, they retreat to deep forest underbrush. In late summer and fall, their feeding enters a frenzy phase, known as hyperphagia. They consume as many as 20,000 calories per day as they prepare for winter hibernation. In this phase, they may be active up to twenty-four hours per day. As they search for food, they readily use human-developed forest trails and roads. Bears also like to frequent stream and riverbeds, avalanche chutes, forest borders, and berry patches.

Most human-bear encounters occur on trails, during the morning and the evening, in the fall and spring. If you sight a bear in the wilderness that doesn't see you, consider it a special treat. If you sight one that does see you, and doesn't run away, prepare to take self-defense actions.

Best practices when hiking in bear country:

▸ Be situationally alert. Note posted warnings of bear activity in your area. Enter trails at trailheads, where you can read current alerts of bear activity.
▸ Hike in a group. The incidence of bear attacks dramatically falls off as the size of a group grows. On the trail, stay together and make noise. Ideally, your noise will alert bears of your presence, and startled bears can be avoided.

Mother grizzly bear and cub

▸ If traveling alone, occasionally clap your hands and yell, "Hey bear!" Click your hiking poles together. Attach bear bells to your pack. While opinions vary on how well these work, in bear-rich country, you are likely to feel more comfortable taking all precautions, including bells, if they are available.

▸ Bear horns are compressed-air-powered horns, similar to boat horns. They produce a loud, sharp sound blast and are easy to use and carry. You could periodically sound a warning blast, but such a practice would ruin everyone's backcountry experience, so save them for when you spot an approaching bear and need to warn it off.

▶ Bear spray is an excellent tool with a strong track record (see page 196). It preserves the bear's life and teaches it to be afraid of humans. Firearms are not practical unless you are highly experienced in their use and have large-game hunting skills. They are also illegal in many park jurisdictions and fatal to the bear.

Bear Encounters

Research biologists differ on appropriate steps to take if the worst happens and you are mauled by a bear. Some say play dead, and others encourage fighting back. Recent research points out that black bears are generally timid, but if they do attack, they intend to kill, and you should fight back with any means possible. Use your fists, a knife, binoculars, bear spray, sticks, or hiking poles.

Grizzly bear attacks have ended after limited mauling. The advice here is to lie facedown, and spread your legs to make it harder to be flipped onto your back, which would expose your stomach. Cover your neck with clasped hands. Continue to wear your backpack, as it will protect your back. Try not to move until the bear is finished. Your goal is to show the grizzly you are not a threat. Certainly, easier said than done.

Camping in Bear County

Do all you can to keep a clean camp. Cook your meals and store your food container at least 100 yards downwind of your campsite. Store food in an approved plastic, bear-proof canister, as well as trash with food smells, cosmetics, sunscreen, toothpaste, and so

Bear Spray

Bear spray and holster

First developed in the 1980s, bear spray has proven to be a highly effective bear deterrent. Research reveals a 98 percent success rate when used correctly. Always carry it in grizzly country.

▸ Store bear spray in a holster where you can easily reach it. Practice a rapid draw. Do not carry it in your pack.

▸ Aim at a charging bear's face. Fire a six-second burst.

▸ Begin spraying when the bear is 30 to 50 feet away. Adjust for wind.

▸ In active bear country, each member of your party should carry spray.

▸ Leave the area immediately after using.

▸ Bear spray cannot be taken on airplanes.

▸ You can often rent it at shops in or near major national parks.

▸ Bear spray is not a repellent like mosquito repellent. Do not spray it on clothes or tents.

▸ Bear spray has an expiration date. Usually good for a few years. Use expired cans for practice.

forth. Do not place the canister in or near your tent. These canisters are increasingly required for camping in backcountry areas.

An alternative is to hang your food in a bag suspended from trees. The goal is to elevate food and odiferous items 15 feet above the ground and 10 feet from the nearest tree. Camping books list numerous methods, but here is a quick one that serves well: Select two trees approximately 25 feet apart, with sturdy branches at least 15 feet off the ground. Tie a carabiner to one end of a 75- to 100-foot piece of paracord. Tie the other end to one of the tree trunks. Throw the carabiner and cord over the first tree's branch. Pull out the cord's slack over the branch. Throw the carabiner over the second tree branch. Midway between each tree, tie a loop in the cord. Attach the food bag to this loop, via an additional carabiner. Lift the bag at least 15 feet off the ground by pulling the cord over the second tree's branch. Tie the cord to the trunk of the second tree. Special bear-proof bags can add to your food security. Ursack-brand bags have a good reputation. Place food in them and hang, as described above.

WILD PIGS

Feral pigs are the dangerous offspring of escaped domestic pigs and European boars. While common in America's Southeast, they are increasingly found in the Western and Southwest US. They breed frequently and can thrive in almost any habitat.

These pigs do substantial damage to agriculture and out-compete native species for food. They are not considered

Wild pig

wildlife and are not native. In most areas, hunting pigs is permitted year-round. Attacks on humans have increased as their populations grow. Typically, this has happened when pigs feel cornered or to protect their young.

If you encounter pigs, most often found in groups of mothers and piglets, move away slowly. Attempt to reach higher ground, such as a boulder. Climb a tree at least six feet off the ground. If attacked, try to remain standing. Fight back with hiking poles or fists, sticks, and rocks. If you are injured, seek medical attention immediately, as pigs are often the carriers of disease. The wounds they cause have a high infection risk.

COYOTES

Coyotes are highly intelligent and extremely adaptable carnivores. They are common in the Western US and are the respected subjects of Native American lore. While preferring open meadows and forest borders, they have increasingly moved into urban areas. They often can be observed, in early morning or evening, in city parks where no other large, wild animals are present. They are prowling and hunting for meadow rodents. Coyotes have an active pack life, and if you see one coyote, others are likely nearby.

Coyote

The behavior of coyotes varies widely, depending on their environment. In forest areas, where they are hunted and trapped, they are usually wary of humans. In suburban areas, they may lose their fear of people. In these areas, domestic pets may become their prey.

Rarely, coyotes have attacked children and adults. Some people walking dogs on leashes have experienced problems. Coyotes will engage unleashed dogs in what appears like play. They have then been known to lure dogs away where they are then attacked and killed by coyote packs.

If coyotes are known to be nearby, protect and monitor small children. If you encounter coyotes, use a loud, authoritative voice to drive them away. Throw rocks or sticks to scare them. If attacked, throw dirt or sand at their eyes.

LIVESTOCK PROTECTION DOGS

A flock of sheep is about as benign and pastoral as one can imagine. And they can be a surprising sight to thru-hikers when encountered across high mountain landscapes. The sheep are there utilizing decades-old US Forest Service grazing rights that often extend into formally designated wilderness areas. The sheep are sometimes protected from predation by aggressive, large dogs known as livestock protection dogs (LPDs). The use of LPDs is less expensive than hiring traditional sheep herders, but the increasing use of these dogs has led to unfortunate human-dog encounters. Hikers have experienced serious bites and even

Working dog sign

fatal maulings. The dogs are various breeds, but often Akbash sheep dogs, beautiful-looking animals that can stand three feet tall and weigh 140 pounds.

If you encounter a sheep flock in your hiking travels, it is best to avoid it. Flocks are usually in open pastures, so it is often easy to circumvent them. Although sheep will move for humans, it is best to not walk through them. The Akbash dog has light-colored fur, and you may not see them within a flock. They may be left on duty without close human supervision. If they spot you, they will bark, raise the hair on their backs, and aggressively approach. Stand your ground. Cool-headed individuals who have encountered them and stood still report that the dogs have sniffed them and then left them alone. Some hikers have raised hiking poles in an attempt to drive dogs away. Reportedly, this has failed and led to further aggression. If you have a bad experience, report it to the appropriate land management agency, usually the US Forest Service.

WOLVES

Gray wolves, also known as timber wolves, are magnificent creatures. While common in Canada and Alaska, they have often been designated a threatened species in the lower forty-eight. In the American West, they can be found in Idaho, Montana, Oregon, Washington, Wyoming, and recently in Colorado. The Mexican wolf is a smaller subspecies of the gray wolf. It was once considered extinct in the wild and has been reintroduced into Arizona and New Mexico.

Gray wolves are large, weighing between 70 and 170 pounds and standing 26 to 40 inches tall. They often eat small rodents, berries, and fruit. But they are apex predators and the most successful of all animals in taking down large game animals. They are more successful in killing powerful moose than are bears or mountain lions. This is due to teamwork developed by hunting in packs. Typically, packs have five to eight members, but can have up to thirty. It is rare to spot a solitary wolf. Expect others to be nearby.

Wolves generally are not aggressive toward humans and attacks are very rare. They are wary of people and do not seek them out. In North America, there are only two documented

Gray wolf

cases of fatalities due to wolves. Wild wolves are rarely a problem. Yellowstone National Park naturalists state that wolf aggression toward visitors is a non-issue. Danger lies with wolves that
have been fed by people and have, otherwise habituated toward
people. Wolf hybrids (semidomesticated wolf-dog mixes) are
actually a greater danger due to their typically close association
with humans.

As wolves are reintroduced in Colorado, New Mexico, Arizona, and some national parks, it is likely that wolf encounters
will become more frequent. As responsible outdoor conserva-
tionists, we should do our part in preventing wolves from becoming habituated to humans.

▸ Avoid leaving food outdoors, including dog food. Never feed wolves.
▸ Observe wolves from a distance. Never approach them.
▸ Avoid den sites.
▸ Notify authorities if you see one near livestock areas or in residential areas.

If you run into wolves, it will likely be a surprise for all parties. Try to remain calm. Breathe deeply. Wolves can sense fear. Try to look large, broaden your shoulders, and stand tall. Do not run. Slowly back away while maintaining eye contact. If the wolf approaches, take one step toward it, make noise, clap, and act aggressively.

If you have a dog with you, leash it. Stay between the dog and the wolf. If the worst happens and you are attacked, fight back. Use rocks and sticks. If you have an air horn or bear spray, use it.

If you drive them off, but suspect they are still around, build a fire. Make it as smoky as possible, using green branches and wet wood. Create a lot of noise, and if you are in a group, keep the group together.

SNAKES

Snakes are common in the Western US. They are valuable creatures because they control small mammal populations. They do not seek to harm humans and prefer to avoid them. Their first

Timber rattlesnake

defense is to rely on camouflage and remain still. Hikers are likely to walk by them without noticing their presence. Hikers with dogs are more prone to encounters. Their second defense is escape. They will attempt to glide away and become lost in underbrush.

Biting is usually a last resort. Of snakes that could bite you, only about 20 percent are poisonous. And of those bites, 25 percent are dry: no venom is injected. In the United States, of the 7,000 to 8,000 individuals bitten in a year, fewer than five die. Those who do are usually the very young or very old.

Rattlesnakes are the poisonous snake hikers are most likely to encounter. They are pit vipers, a category of snakes that includes rattlesnakes, copperheads, and water moccasins. All have distinct triangular heads and catlike pupils. Despite the name, not all rattlesnakes have rattles. And rattlesnakes do not always rattle when disturbed. Rattlesnakes are more active in spring and fall. They seek out spots that are exposed to morning sun. They prefer rocky spots, river bottoms, brush heaps, and old logs.

There are a few precautions hikers can take. Wear ankle-high boots. Gaiters are helpful. In extreme snake habitat, thick, tall snake gaiters may be worn. As you hike, focus on the trail ahead. Do not wear earbuds. Instead, listen for rattles. If you hear one, freeze. Find the snake with your eyes. Wait for it to relax. And then slowly back away.

If you are bitten, try to remain calm. Emotional and physical agitation increases the effect of envenomation (a snake bite where venom is injected). Note the time of the bite. Remove rings and watches that will hamper circulation if swelling occurs. Wash the bite spot. Stay well hydrated. Contrary to popular myth, do not cut open the wound, apply a tourniquet, or attempt to suck out the venom. Do not try to capture the snake for examination. Instead, take a photo or form a visual memory of its appearance. If you are stable, slowly walk out, keeping your heart rate low, resting frequently, and drinking water. Venomous poison can cause a wide range of symptoms. They include swelling, pain, nausea, and blurred vision. If you are reacting to the venom, seek evacuation assistance. In all cases, obtain medical treatment, preferably from a facility that has antivenom on hand.

THE REST OF THE STORY . . .

While processing the mother bear's renewed attack, I unholstered my can of bear spray and held it ready in my hand. When the bear was about 30 feet away, I released a spray directly toward her face. She did an amazing pirouette and vanished in a flash back into the forest. My training, which was to deliver short bursts of the spray, failed me as my adrenaline took hold. I continued emptying the can with a shaking arm well after the bear was gone.

13

Communication Safety Tools

DON'T LET THIS HAPPEN TO YOU

One would be hard-pressed to find two more experienced hikers than Elizabeth and Dan. Longtime outdoor instructors, naturalists, and gear experts, the two often meet up on days off work to work on challenging backcountry routes. A current project is to complete the entire Continental Divide Trail (CDT) from Canada to Mexico, a few segments at a time.

One of the most remote sections of the CDT is located in New Mexico's Carson National Forest. The trail is often not marked, and navigation skills are required to hike the CDT. Elizabeth and Dan used a GPS mapping system on their cell phones. The area is beautiful, and for several days, the hikers made good time. They were backpacking the first weeks of June, and it had been an exceptionally snowy spring. They encountered only two other hikers during the first four days of the trip. The higher elevation sections of the trail were still buried in snow or were covered with

Electronics come to the wilderness.

two or three inches of standing water (snowmelt), so there was no visible trail to follow for long distances. GPS software enabled them to stay on the course, but it used a lot of battery power.

Elizabeth and Dan were deep in the wilderness, far from anywhere when their cell phones eventually indicated drained batteries. They expected this to happen and wisely packed a fully charged power bank and backup paper maps. Unfortunately, Elizabeth packed the wrong power cord, so they could not recharge the phones. Then they realized their paper maps didn't show the exit trail cutoff to New Mexico's historic Ghost Ranch, where their car was parked.

OUTDOOR-FOCUSED ELECTRONICS are rapidly evolving. Smartwatches, cell phones, satellite phones, two-way radios, satellite-based Global Positioning System devices, and personal locater beacons have demonstrated success in keeping hikers "found," signaling for emergency help and providing specific navigational coordinates to rescuers. Manufacturers highlight the many lives saved by these devices.

Less common to hear about are the numerous times these various devices have failed. All are dependent on batteries and transmission distances, which are subject to limitations. Cold weather drains battery power. Signals are blocked by canyon walls and mountain ranges. Tree canopies, wind, and snow interfere with reception.

In many situations, it is valuable for hikers to carry these devices. However, a common admonition is that it is a good practice to always back up these devices with a map, a compass, and the skills to use them. Wiser advice is to know first how to use a map and compass and to consider electronic devices as your backups.

WATCHES

A simple, rugged field watch, such as a Swiss Army watch, is a useful addition to your travel safety. A watch can identify when you have reached your turnaround time, help you know how much daylight you have before nightfall, and clarify if you are closing in on the time you identified when friends or family are to notify the sheriff that you are overdue. If you are trained in Wilderness First Aid, a watch allows you to measure key vital signs of an injured hiking partner, including heart and respiratory rates. Watches can be helpful navigation tools by letting you know your speed of travel to major landmarks.

ABC Field Watches

These robust, battery-powered field watches have several useful, basic features, including an altimeter, barometer, and compass (ABC). An ABC watch is a good choice as a backup for a nonelectronic compass. The barometer feature can alert you to dramatically changing air pressure and approaching storms. The altimeter is useful in confirming topographical map locations. However, the displayed altitude can vary up to 1,000 feet, depending on air pressure. They work best when you update altitude settings frequently. Reset them when you are at known-

Calibrating Altimeters

Flying into an airport near your hiking destination? Consider hanging back as the plane empties and asking the pilot for the present altitude of the aircraft. The plane's superior altimeter will provide a highly precise altitude reading by which to set your ABC watch.

altitude landmarks, which show up on your map, such as lakes, trailheads, and passes.

The batteries in ABC watches can last for over a year, depending on how frequently you use the compass and altimeter. Often, they are designed so you can easily change the battery in the field, and typically have an indicator to warn you when a battery is running low.

Smartwatches

Smartwatches, such as the Apple Watch or Garmin Fenix, can be highly useful devices. They house dozens of functions, many of which can be beneficial to hikers and mountaineers. They are the next step up from ABC watches, both in features and complication. Their major contribution is the addition of GPS location tracking and fitness and health-monitoring sensors. Additional applications are continually being developed. Many of these require pairing the watch with a nearby smartphone. Safety-related features may include heart rate, blood-oxygen level, EKG rhythm, and skin temperature monitoring. Some can serve as a flashlight, be used as a walkie-talkie, send SOS calls, and receive weather alerts.

Cell phones have many of the same functions, but a smart-watch on your wrist is more readily accessible and, therefore, more likely to be consulted. Note that its many virtues also require substantial battery power and daily recharging. Some newer models can function for up to a week or more with careful use. Recently, solar-powered versions are available.

CELL PHONES

Of all the electronic devices this chapter reviews, cell phones have proven to be the most useful backcountry tool for locating those lost or injured. They are readily available, and you are wise to carry one on your hikes.

Backcountry travel can be rough on electronic devices. Carry your phone in a zippered pocket or carrier and protect it from moisture. In cold weather, carry it under your outer layer. Allowing it to get too cold can drain the battery, rendering it useless for the rest of the trip.

On the way to the trailhead, top off its charge from your vehicle's battery. Try to begin your trip with your phone as fully charged as possible. At your starting point, make sure your phone's automatic location setting is enabled. This generates the "pings" that rescuers can use to locate your position. When not in use, turn your phone off to conserve energy. Occasionally, turn your phone back on for a minimum of five minutes. The phone will search for the nearest cell phone tower and, ideally, leave an electronic footprint of your location. Most phones also have a low-battery or airplane mode, useful for preserving battery life.

Technology has a tendency to fail us when we need it most. Large areas of the American West and most of the earth's surface do not have cell service. If you do not have a signal, try climbing to a nearby ridge or peak. Cell phones work by line of sight, and the higher you are, the better. Their signals can be blocked by rock features and dense forest vegetation. Active snowstorms and high winds also distort signals.

Since cell phones are at their strongest when they first acquire a signal, try toggling in and out of airplane mode if you don't have reception. This will also force a phone without reception to look for the best signal.

Colorado's Alpine Rescue Team has discovered that weak signals can also be blocked by the density of the caller's head. When you are trying to call, they advise setting your phone on speaker mode and holding it as high as you can above your head.

If you encounter a nonresponsive individual in need of help who has an iPhone, you can go to the locked screen and there, tap "emergency." Medical ID also appears. This service, available only in the US, will allow you access to the owner's stored emergency medical information, such as chronic conditions and emergency contacts, if set up.

SATELLITE PHONES

Hand-held mobile satellite phones are generally reliable and will work anywhere in the world, as long as a communication satellite is visible to them. They can be expensive and require service subscriptions. They are not commonly used by domestic hikers. They are most frequently used by expeditions, scientists, researchers, and guides. Their use, in some countries, requires permits or is illegal altogether. Their great advantage is that they also allow extensive two-way communication and the ability to call 911 directly. They can be complicated to use, so if you decide to carry one, practice with it well in advance of any emergency situation where it may be required. It is also possible to rent satellite phones for short-term use.

FAMILY RADIO SERVICE RADIOS

Family Radio Service (FRS) radios are hand-held, battery-operated two-way radios, also known as walkie-talkies. Their range is line of sight and very limited in rugged country. They are inexpensive and popular with groups. They serve well with hiking clubs, which often place one with the front leader and one with the rear leader.

Better models often include NOAA weather-alert capabilities. If you purchase an FRS radio, buy a model with a scan feature. This allows the radio to search channels and connect to other users in range. These individuals are likely close enough to offer emergency help. You can also try broadcasting for help on channel 20, informally considered the FRS emergency channel. If you are unable to establish any contact, do not hesitate to broadcast "in the blind." Your signal may be heard even if you cannot hear others.

SATELLITE MESSENGER SYSTEMS

In an emergency, calling for help with your cell phone is a good first choice. However, its ability to communicate is limited by the nearness of earth-bound cell phone towers, often not available in backcountry locations.

Space-based satellite-facilitated systems dramatically increase your ability to communicate. With a few exceptions, their range covers the entire planet. Two choices of satellite rescue devices exist for sending distress signals: personal locator beacons and satellite emergency notification devices. Study your options carefully. Your life may depend on it.

Personal Locator Beacons

When you purchase a personal locator beacon (PLB), you must register it with NOAA's Search and Rescue Satellite-Aided Tracking (SARSAT) database. You provide phone numbers, address, and emergency contact information. Beyond the purchase price of the beacon, there is no fee for registration, nor a service contract.

Deployed personal locator beacon

Satellite Emergency Notification Devices

Satellite emergency notification devices (SEND) provide features beyond calling for rescue. These include the ability to send custom messages to friends and family, such as "I am OK," or "I will be out one day longer." Some can also send limited text messages.

SEND units use GPS satellites for location finding and commercial networks for communication. SEND devices transmit signals in the 0.4- and 1.6-watt range. When an emergency distress signal is sent, it is routed through GEOS International Emergency Response Center, a private corporation located in Houston,

Texas. The Center will attempt to reach you and also contact SAR services near your location.

SEND manufacturers continue to develop services for their devices. These include topo map displays, waypoint tracking, Bluetooth pairing with your cell phone, and weather reports. These features come at a price. Beyond the cost of the device, activation and monthly subscription fees are often required. The added features limit battery life. Users report ranges from one to twenty days.

PLB Versus SEND

A healthy debate exists among users of the two types of devices. All have saved lives, and all have failed in emergencies. Operator error has been shown to be a cause for some device failure. If you are considering purchasing a satellite device, first check social and commercial sites for recent, real-world user reviews of the wide-ranging pros and cons of the various models. Consider battery life, emergency call functions, and ease of use in a crisis situation as key priorities in your choice. Remember that the use of these devices also reduces the risk to the rescuers who are called to your aid.

HAM RADIOS

An additional communication option exists, and it is one you may have not considered. Ham radios, or two-meter amateur radios, are the radios you see being used by SAR rescue teams. Colorado's Alpine Rescue Team also recommends them as a good choice for civilian backcountry use.

These handheld radios are easy to use, relatively lightweight, and inexpensive. They have a line-of-sight range of about 100 miles. This is enhanced by numerous repeater sites often placed and maintained by amateur radio enthusiasts. A federal license

Carry Park Phone Numbers

My wife and I kayaked to a remote wilderness campsite in Grand Teton National Park, in northern Wyoming. During the night, she lost orientation to events, location, and time. It was a scary and rare condition later diagnosed in the hospital as transitory amnesia. I called 911 on my cell phone. The message "skipped" to a 911 call center in southern Wyoming. They routed my information through a central communication hub in the state capitol, where the information was forwarded to the Grand Teton National Park dispatch. While the process eventually worked, it took extra time and had the potential to lose key information.

In hindsight, I should have known that the National Park Service handles their own rescues, and I would have saved valuable time by calling the Teton Interagency Dispatch Center number. Park emergency numbers are written on park websites, backcountry permit forms, and park newspapers. I would have been wise to enter the number into my cell phone contacts before heading into the backcountry.

is required to operate them. Online study guides, practice tests, and multiple-choice test format facilitate obtaining your license. These materials are available through the American Radio Relay League at arrl.org. No license is required for emergency use.

BATTERIES—FOR BETTER OR WORSE

Battery-operated devices are now a routine part of one's backcountry equipment—headlamps, locator beacons, watches, weather radios, cell phones, GPS devices, ultraviolet water purifiers, and cameras, all of which can have positive safety-related purposes.

Always start your trip with fresh batteries and carry spares. Half-used batteries can be saved for front country and household purposes that are not safety critical. If possible, attempt to standardize the types of batteries you use so you have interchangeability in the field. Standard-size AA batteries are a good choice. They will last two times as long as smaller AAA batteries and are similar in expense. Be sure to fully charge any devices with rechargeable batteries.

Protect devices and batteries from cold and heat. Alkaline batteries are readily available and, if forgotten, can be picked up at convenience stores on the way to the trailhead. They slowly decline in performance as they discharge, warning you of their impending end.

Lithium batteries are less common and more expensive. Unlike alkaline batteries, they still work well in cold temperatures. They maintain consistent voltage over their lifespan and

How to Call for Medical Help

If you have decided that you cannot resolve your emergency with existing resources, cannot self-rescue, and must call for help, follow these steps:

▸ Realize your call time may be limited or cut short.

▸ Rehearse what you will say, writing down key information you need to share.

▸ Early in your conversation, state your name and the exact location of the injured individual.

▸ Be specific in what assistance you are requesting, for example medical personnel, mountain rescue, evacuation, or helicopter.

▸ Share the time of the accident or incident.

▸ Share the nature and extent of any injuries.

▸ Share your cell phone number in case their equipment did not capture it.

▸ Report what survival gear you have, such as first aid kit, sleeping bag, tarp, and any relevant medical training group members have: for example nurse, Wildness First Responder, and so forth.

then rapidly quit. They are usually the best choice for devices needing consistent power. For ultralight hikers, they have the advantage of weighing significantly less than other batteries.

Lithium-ion (Li-on) batteries are usually those found in cameras, smartphones, and battery chargers. They also work well in the cold. They are often nonstandard sizes and can be difficult to replace in the field.

NiMH rechargeable batteries reduce waste and can be used many times. They slowly discharge when left on the shelf at home, so be sure to give them a fresh charge before your trip.

Conserving Battery Life

SAR staff report that all too often, when they get a call for help, one of the first things the missing party informs them is that they have very little cell phone battery power left. This is not a situation you want to find yourself in.

GPS, cameras, trail apps, and mapping apps use significant battery power. Take proactive steps to conserve battery power by doing the following:

1. Turning on your cell phone's power-saving mode.
2. Using airplane mode when you do not need network data.
3. Turning down the brightness of your smartphone screen. It is a particularly heavy user of battery power.
4. Closing apps you are not using.
5. If you are with a group dealing with an emergency, turning off all cell phones but one.

Disposing of Batteries

Today, most used batteries can be recycled. The Environmental Protection Agency states that household batteries should not go in household garbage or recycling bins. Instead, inquire at your local big-box hardware store or office supply store. The website Earth911.com can match your zip code with the nearest recycling center that accepts various types of batteries.

THE REST OF THE STORY . . .

Elizabeth and Dan continued to travel on their route using paper maps, navigation skills, and a monocle to depart from the trail and make their way toward Ghost Ranch. They camped by a river that night, and then, they got lucky! They encountered a fly-fisherman. Elizabeth asked if he had a charging cord they could borrow. She offered to sit on the bank while he fished, and they charged their phone from their battery pack. The fisherman kindly gave them the cord and became part of the happy ending to their trip.

Backcountry Street Smarts

DON'T LET THIS HAPPEN TO YOU

Friends spent a great weekend at a backcountry snowshoe-in cabin, enjoying good food, good weather, and good conversation. The hike out brought them back to the parking lot around 1:00 p.m. It was then that smiles turned to frowns when they noticed shattered glass shards on the ground. Unfortunately, it was from their car.

WE HAVE LEARNED to protect ourselves in a front country urban environment. We know not to visit certain crime-prone areas alone, and we have developed a sixth sense about avoiding someone on the street if we feel uncomfortable. If the worst happens, we know to call 911 and can quickly summon law enforcement or fire rescue personnel. And we know that twenty-four-hour advanced emergency medical care is always available.

Left: Trailhead theft warning sign **Right:** Trailhead car damage

As are poison hotlines, natural gas leak responders, and all-night tow trucks. These skills develop over time and become second nature to use.

The backcountry has its own set of dangers. The difference is few of us grew up in that environment. We need to deliberately educate ourselves to the unique challenges of the wilderness. We can learn the skills we need through courses and handbooks such as this one. And the good news is, the same intuition you use in the city can become attuned to the special dangers of the backcountry.

TRAILHEAD BREAK-INS

Nothing ruins a terrific hike more than returning to find your car with a broken window and you or a companion a victim of theft. Regrettably, as trail use increases, vehicle break-ins are growing. Remote trailheads accessible by dirt or gravel roads have the fewest incidents. More common are break-ins near cities with nearby highway access. Parking spots near ski areas are also particularly subject to thieves.

No vehicles are immune. But there are steps you can take to help protect your valuables while you are hiking and exploring the backcountry.

1. **Be alert to high-theft areas.** Crime-plagued parking spots often have signs posted, warning of theft. Review hiking blogs and trail websites for recent reports of thefts. When parking, look for signs of crime, such as broken glass on the ground. Auto-window glass usually shatters in small, rounded shards.

2. **Park defensively.** If available, park under street lighting. Spots nearest the start of the trail, outhouses, or trail kiosks have the most foot traffic and discourage thieves.

3. **Lock your car.** This step is often overlooked when busily gearing up to hit the trail. Check all windows and the sunroof. Placing an obvious, bright-colored bar lock on your steering wheel discourages thieves.

4. **Keep items left in your car out of sight.** It is never wise to leave valuables in your car, but if you must, put them in the trunk or under seating. Common theft targets are cell phones, chargers, sunglasses, clothing, or loose change.

5. **Remove your vehicle registration from your glove box or leave a version without an address on it.** Hikers have reported being subject to break-ins where the crooks stole garage door openers and addresses from registrations left in vehicles. Knowing the owners are out on the trail and not at home, the thieves compound the misery by quickly driving to the victims' home and robbing it as well.

   If you are a victim, report it to law enforcement. Trailheads are often in rural areas covered by sheriff's departments. Typically, they have twenty-four-hour nonemergency numbers where you can file a report. Reporting will not restore your damage, but it is often required for insurance purposes. And it might generate extra patrols or postings, which could help other potential victims.

CRIME ON THE TRAIL

There is not much research on the incidence of trail crime, but what does exist suggests you are much safer—crime-wise—on a wilderness trail than in urban parks or on city streets. Common sense tends to support this premise. Hikers are not attractive victims for thieves. Few hikers carry valuables. Their travel is unpredictable and infrequent. Plus, hikers tend to be fit, confident, and aware of their surroundings. They are not the most vulnerable individuals nor in a typical location for criminal victimization. Where on-trail incidents have occurred, they are usually close to parking lots or roads.

Dangerous backcountry exceptions are marijuana groves, methamphetamine processors, and moonshine stills. These are often protected, sometimes with trip wires or armed guards. Although hidden in forests, the surrounding area will often contain items such as PVC pipe, fertilizer containers, fake private property signs, trash, and camouflage netting. Despite increasing drug legalization, economics still dictate an underground black market for drugs, and these sites continue to be established in remote locations.

If you encounter such a spot, leave immediately. Do not take photos. You may be observed and thus, endanger yourself. When safely away, write down the site location and any detail you can recall. Report your find to law enforcement. Your action may prevent a future hiker from being harmed.

Preventing Personal Assault

Be situationally aware, paying attention to others in the area. On remote trails, it is fairly easy to discover footprints that can reveal if others were present recently. Your instincts are a good warning system as well. If something "feels wrong," it may well be.

Be courteous to those you encounter. Avoid confrontations. Be alert to those not equipped as hikers. Carry a cell phone and know if you have coverage.

If you are a victim:

▸ Try to remain calm.
▸ Give up the items asked for. Your life is more important.
▸ Fight back if attacked.
▸ After an incident, leave the area.
▸ Contact the local sheriff's office or a park ranger.
▸ Write down a description of the thieves, any vehicle description, license number, and direction of travel.
▸ Save, but if possible, do not handle, evidence of the crime.

Observing a Crime

If you think you have observed a crime, do not approach the perpetrator or take their photo. Remember key observations, write them down and report to authorities. Law enforcement officers will ask you for descriptions of people involved, their vehicles, and any distinguishing logos, license plates, or car rental identifiers.

TWO-LEGGED ANIMALS

A national survey of hikers asked what they were most fearful of on backcountry trails, for example bears, lightning, forest fires, and so on. Somewhat surprising to the surveyors, the overwhelming answer was "two-legged animals." While troubling, perhaps such an answer should not be unexpected. In a time when dictators invade peaceful countries, pandemics are spread by personal contact, and crime statistics are dramatically increasing, it may be that our fellow humans are our biggest threat.

Fortunately, while there are cases of trail crime and assaults, they are very rare. Millions of hiking trips occur each year in the Western US, and crimes occur only on a miniscule portion of them.

Our fears may not be warranted, but they can persist. Perhaps this is because, in our primitive past, the forest was a place of life-threatening dangers. Cave bears hunted our ancestors, and prehistoric tribes attacked one another to gain power, bolster provisions, and take prisoners for trade or slavery. Sounds in the night or in remote locations alert us, and our minds imagine the worst.

Handling Fear

From the perspective of safety skills, a certain amount of fear can be a positive emotion. It makes us attentive to our environment and mindful of reactions to it. It leads us to be cautious in difficult backcountry situations, which is a healthy reaction.

It is typical to experience many strong emotions in the wilderness. Positive ones include awe and a sense of beauty, joy, and peace. Negative ones include dread, panic, and anxiety. This range of emotions is normal, and we all experience a limited amount of each at some time. They become safety issues if they overcome us and interfere with our hiking experiences and relationships.

Psychologists recognize that the forest is a powerful stimulus. They have defined the condition of hylophobia as an irrational fear of the forest. Nyctohylophobia is the fear of forests at night. Such anxiety events can be debilitating for a hiker and need to be addressed. Leading wilderness medicine courses and textbooks have acknowledged the need for an open, responsive dialogue around mental health and have added mental health content and patient-support methodology within the last few years.

If your fears move beyond a constructive usefulness, consultation with mental health professionals is a constructive step. They can assist with desensitization techniques, self-help techniques, and guided meditation. Current methodologies can include neurolinguistic programming and cognitive behavioral therapy.

SOLO HIKING

Hiking solo is the source of much debate. Clearly, hiking with others has many safety advantages. There is someone to nurse a partner's injury and go for help if necessary. With a companion, you have double the equipment and resources in an emergency. Fewer wildlife encounters happen with a larger group. Multiple sets of eyes can watch for trail markers or dangerous hazards.

There are also social advantages to hiking with others. Rich conversation can occur, and there is the joy and bonding of shared experiences. Conversely, best friends in the city may find extended time together on the trail trying. Dehydration, steep trails, and heavy packs may bring out a different side of you or

Tips for Solo Hiking and Camping

▶ Over-plan, but don't over-pack.

▶ Learn the safety skills in this book.

▶ Identify bail-out points on your map. Use them if trouble develops.

▶ Know that it is *always* OK to turn around.

▶ Consider carrying a PLB or satellite device. It will give you confidence, even if you never use it.

▶ If you encounter someone who makes you uncomfortable, you do not have to be nice. Confident body language can be an effective deterrent. Stand tall, with shoulders back and head up.

▶ Camp at least a mile from the road. This decreases your likelihood of encountering other people.

▶ Start with short solo outings where you know the environment is safe. Local trails and state parks are often good choices as they often have safety regulations and are well policed. As your confidence builds, expand your adventures.

▶ Hike with a dog.

your partner. The trail term for this is "expedition fever." This sometimes can lead to hiking partners splitting up on the trail, which is the source of some major backcountry disasters, even when both parties agree to it. Avoid separating if at all possible.

While solo hiking is demonstrably riskier, some enjoy the solitude and even prefer it. Your decisions are your own, you have no need to rush, and you can get started as early or as late as you like. Escaping workday stress is often cited as a reason for hiking. If you deal with others daily from 9:00 a.m. to 5:00 p.m., a solitary backcountry trip can be just the tonic your psyche needs. Sometimes it is the only choice you have, as it can be difficult to find partners, especially midweek, last-minute, and as you age.

If going solo is the right choice for you, take extra care in your preparations. Think through as many emergency contingencies as you can imagine and prepare for them. Be sure to "Leave a Trace" of your itinerary with responsible individuals (see Appendix D).

Study the weather forecasts in great detail. Stick to trails that you are comfortable with, saving the more challenging or exploratory trails for when friends or family can accompany you.

THE REST OF THE STORY . . .

The county sheriff's deputy responded quickly to the friend's call. She shared there had been a rash of break-ins in the area. The thieves had developed refined tactics. They hid in the forest, well away from the car they intended to rob. Using an air rifle, they shot out the targeted car window. If an alarm was triggered, they were out of view from any passerby. If there was no alarm, they were free to begin their thieving.

Epilogue
MANAGING AN INCIDENT

With hiking comes risk. While you can never alleviate all risk, you can absolutely learn to prepare for and manage it. Educating yourself by reading this and other books, taking courses, and talking in advance with your group about responsibilities should an incident occur are key.

Most major outdoor clubs provide seminars, classes, and field schools, where students can not only study in the classroom but also actually experience dealing with common wilderness emergencies through staged emergency scenarios. But while all this training is crucial, the fact is, it can be difficult to remember all that you were trained to do—and correctly apply that training—in the chaos of a real-life emergency situation.

Assigning leaders and having a system are all part of the key steps necessary to stabilize an unplanned wilderness incident. Preparation starts with getting your whole hiking group on board with the same plan. Whether in a formal hiking group or part of an on-off informal meetup among casual friends, all mindful hiking partners should take a few moments at the trailhead to discuss safety matters. This ideally includes the weather forecast, turnaround times, any expected challenging trail conditions and fall exposure, the nearest emergency medical services, and the steps to take if someone in the group can't keep up or has to leave for any reason. Trailhead briefings are especially important if the group includes novices or children.

It's important to agree in advance on who will do what should an incident occur. Who is your trip leader? This person is the one undertaking overall guidance and continued leadership throughout the trip, usually including things like scheduling, transportation arrangements, and route selection.

Should an incident occur, who is your decision-maker? That's your incident commander. This person engages in big-picture oversight of unexpected incidents that may occur on the trip. This could include medical- or illness-related events, such as altitude sickness, hypothermia, or injury. Incidents could include a missing group member or members who become separated from the group or stranded. The trip leader can also serve as incident commander, but it's even better if the tasks are assigned to two different individuals. Typically, these are the two most experienced group members.

Who is prepared to be your group's first aid lead? This is usually the member of the group who has the most advanced medical training. In larger groups, there is often a physician, nurse, or Wilderness First Responder among them. Useful first aid leaders include obvious choices, such as a physician, nurse, or Wilderness First Responder; however, other good options might be EMTs, physical therapists, certified nursing assistants, ski patrollers, and those with Wilderness First Aid training.

Several secondary roles can be assigned in order to take the pressure off the key roles. For example, one member can take the lead on how best to get help, such as figuring out what communication resources are available among the group (phones, PLBs, radios) or making plans for a hike-out team if electronic means are impossible. Someone can assist the first aid lead, recording vital signs or searching the injured party's pack for a first aid kit or personal information card. This frees the first aid

Personal Information Form

Carrying a personal information card, with your contact information and key personal history, is crucial. You can use published forms or simply create one of your own. It should be filled out in advance of any trip you take and carried in your personal first aid kit. Include your name, weight, blood type, full address, and the address and phone numbers of emergency contacts. Add relevant medical history, current medications, known allergies, and primary care doctor. Consider asking your group in advance to have this information on their person, as well, before heading out. Having this card is important to first aid providers, particularly in case of an unresponsive patient.

lead to address the patient's life threats and conduct hands-on assessments. Another member can take charge of planning for an overnight stay should that become necessary, including surveying group members for available bivy equipment, such as tarps and sleeping bags, selecting possible shelter locations, and gathering fire-making materials.

Information in managing incidents is often included in first aid and safety courses. Risk managers are increasingly recognizing the value of dedicated field classes on the topic. Consider attending a Wilderness First Aid class as your next step.

ACKNOWLEDGMENTS

This book builds upon the work of a century of Colorado Mountain Club members, trip leaders, instructors, and staff who came before me. They led the way in facilitating safe backcountry travel and innovative educational offerings.

Special recognition to Linda Lawson for championing and mentoring the CMC safety culture. Instructors who contributed ideas, research, and inspiration include Dan Peterson, John Lindner, Jeff Flax, Kevin Schaal, Robbie Monsma, Rich McAdams, and Joe Griffith.

Helpful subject editing was provided by Roger Wendell, Robin Commons, Dave Ruscitto from Douglas County SAR, Bruce Beckmann from Alpine SAR, Andreas Vogel, Steve Billig, Elizabeth Maroney, Dan Peterson, Rolf Asphaug, wildland firefighter David C., and the US Forest Service.

My deepest gratitude to the CMC Hiking Safety Seminar Team of Steve Billig, Elizabeth Maroney, Tom Hartzell, and Tammy Cullins for their support, dedication, and contribution of wisdom.

As always, heartfelt thanks to Mary Bradley, CMC Denver Group liaison, who assisted this project and me in countless ways.

Photographs were contributed by Steve Billig, Mary Bradley, Elizabeth Maroney, Frank Bursynski, Adam Johanknecht, Frank Biasi, Sanjay Tyagi, Jon Kedrowski, and Ellen Nelson.

Volunteer subjects included Derek Kimmerle, Liana Giacherio, Danielle Serra, Carol Kotchek, Hana Hamilton, Riley Hanlon, Graham Ottley, Sarah Gorecki, Captain Sanjay Tyagi, and Lieutenant Greg Veltri.

The high-quality professional drawings were created by Margaret DeLuca from Alpine SAR.

Bentgate Mountaineering of Golden, Colorado, provided clothing and technical assistance.

Publication expertise was kindly shared by Philip Yancey, David Hachmeister, and L. J. Hachmeister.

Highly competent editing and guidance was provided by Sarah Gorecki, CMC chief publishing officer; Casey Blaine, editor; and Gretel Hakanson, copyeditor. Their professionalism, knowledge, and brilliance made this a special project.

And my deepest of all gratitude, respect, and love to my wife, Sydney, without whose support, experience, editing, and caring this book would not exist.

Appendix A
THE BARGAIN TEN ESSENTIALS: EQUIPMENT FOR ANY BUDGET

In hiking safety seminars, CMC instructors sometimes empty their own packs and share the Ten Essentials they routinely carry on hikes. These instructors have usually been climbers and hikers for decades and have fine-tuned their equipment and acquired some high-quality items.

Upon seeing that equipment, it's not unusual for new hikers to worry they cannot afford the level of gear instructors have gathered over many years. Their concerns may be heightened from reading trip itineraries that routinely require all participants to carry the Ten Essentials. No one wants to stand out by being ill-equipped.

In the spirit of being welcoming and inclusive to all hikers, instructors have created a Ten Essentials list that is lower cost and meets the requirements for supporting safety in the wilderness. The following gear recommendations have been tested in the field and found suitable for easy and moderate hikes.

1. Shelter

A temporary emergency shelter will help you survive an unplanned, though maybe uncomfortable, night out. While commercially produced bivouac bags or thermal tarps work well, low-cost alternatives are large, black trash bags. The best are heavy-duty contractor bags. Larger and stronger than regular trash bags, they work best if you place your legs and torso in one and your upper body in the second, cutting a slit hole for your head.

Contactor bags are sold in large boxes that contain more than one person will ever need. Contactors will often give you a few at no cost. These bags can also serve as rain covers for your pack, which will keep your gear dry. In the sun, they can be used to melt snow for drinking water. Trash compactor bags are a good alternative—they are thick and won't puncture easily.

2. Sun Protection

It is likely you already have sunglasses. Take them year-round. Sunscreen is also necessary. Special mountain sunscreen is not required if you have a generic brand with a high SPF level and it is relatively new. Sunscreen can lose its effectiveness after a couple of years.

3. Navigation

A compass, a backup, and the knowledge to use them is invaluable. Get one with a clear, flat base plate, which is a key to locating north and setting and finding field bearings. The backup compass can be very basic, such as one attached to a key chain or thermometer. Also, many cell phones have a compass feature. This can serve as your backup, if you are in satellite range. Check to make sure it is calibrated properly before you head out on the trail.

A cell phone can also serve as a secondary navigation device. The free Gaia GPS app shows your location using the phone's satellite access. Free maps can be printed from your home computer from websites such as CalTopo.com or GaiaGPS.com.

4. Nutrition/Hydration

A typical trail lunch is a sandwich augmented with trail mix and salty snacks. Carry a couple of sport bars in case you are stuck overnight. Electrolyte packets or tablets are lightweight and useful because they add electrolytes, antioxidants, and essential nutrients to water.

Two or three liters of water are usually adequate for a day hike. Used 32-ounce Gatorade bottles are lightweight, have a large mouth (easy to clean), and will last all hiking season. They are free after your initial purchase of the drink and popular with long-distance hikers practicing ultralight techniques. Water purification tablets, such as Potable Aqua, are less costly than a filter and useful if you need to replenish your original water supply from a spring or stream.

5. Insulation

It is wise to have extra clothes in reserve. A wool or fleece "watch cap" should go with you on any mountain trip, all year long. Spare socks can serve as mittens in an emergency. Rain gear, top and bottom, is necessary, but can be pricey. Frogg Toggs are an exception. This simple jacket and pants set is at a price level unlike any other rain gear. In 2022, new ultralight Frogg Toggs rainsuits were available at Amazon for $20.00. This gear is thin and must be handled carefully, but Frogg Toggs have gained a cult following among long-distance hikers, who swear by their products. They have survived many 2,000-mile-plus long-distance hikes. It is also wise to carry a lightweight down jacket. In recent years, the quality of these items has improved to where even low-cost ones will serve well. In 2022, several name-brand outfitters carried good quality down jackets for under $60.

6. Illumination

Most any kind of flashlight is adequate to get you started. Headlamps are preferred, as they can be used hands-free. Sports outlet stores often carry last year's models at a deeply discounted price. The least expensive models available online today are far better than the most expensive models from five years ago.

7. First Aid

Beginning day hikers can get by with a simple prepackaged kit, which can be found at outdoors stores and online. Add to it three days' worth of any prescription medication you take. A small bottle of hand sanitizer can also be added in order to disinfect wounds, serve as a fire starter, and clean your hands. Hand sanitizer can also be used to remove tree sap from hands, clothing, or hair.

8. Fire Starter

A BIC-type butane cigarette lighter can be purchased cheaply at a convenience store. Back it up with self-striking wooden matches in a waterproof container, such as a used, plastic medicine bottle.

You can create fire starters, which are useful for starting materials in moist conditions, by bundling a dozen wooden matches and dipping the head in melted candle wax. Cotton balls coated with Vaseline and stored in a zip-top bag also work well. Carry a pocket comb? They light easily and provide a strong flame for emergency fire starting.

9. Repair Kit

A small Swiss Army knife will do and can be found for under $20. It will serve many purposes and contains repair features such as a screwdriver head and scissors. A small roll of duct tape will mend torn clothing and shelters as well as help stabilize broken hiking poles and wrenched wrists. If you have a big roll at home, wind several feet around your water bottle or hiking pole.

10. Communication

The sound of a whistle will carry much farther than a human can shout for rescue. Three whistle blasts mean "HELP!" One blast in response, means "I am coming to help." (See Appendix C for more details.) A quality whistle can be purchased for as little as $2.00.

Appendix B
BASIC FIRST AID KIT

The content of a first aid kit should vary with the length of the trip, the number in the group, and the expected environment, for example aquatic, desert, forest, or mountain. Kits should be refreshed after each trip. If you have not used your kit in a while, review its contents before your next outing. This will allow you to perform more efficiently in treating an injury under difficult circumstances.

Ideally, each individual will carry their own kit tailored to their specific needs. Wilderness First Aid protocols direct that the patient's own first aid supplies are used first in their treatment. Their kit will be opened by trained rescuers in search of a personal medical information form, in the case of a nonresponsive patient.

Basic First Aid Kit

WHAT	HOW MANY	WHY
Nitrile gloves	2 pair	Reduce bacteria transfer
Band-Aids	12	Care of minor wounds
Gauze pads 2"×2"	6	Large wounds
Gauze pads 3"×4"	2	Larger wounds
Gauze pads 4"×4"	2	Larger wounds
Adhesive skin bandages	6	Close wound
▸ Gauze roll, 3" wide	1	Compress, hold bandages
▸ Adhesive tape, 2" wide	1	Wrap sprains
▸ Triangle bandage	2	Sling injured arm
▸ Moleskin	6" square	Blisters
▸ Alcohol swabs	4	Clean skin
▸ Double antibiotic ointment	2 tubes	Antiseptic
▸ Iodine swabs	4	Antiseptic
▸ Aspirin	6 tablets	Pain, headache
▸ Acetaminophen	6 tablets	Pain, headache, aspirin allergy
▸ Antihistamine	2 tablets	Itch reduction
▸ Insect bite wipes	4	Itch reduction
▸ Pocket rescue mask	1	CPR
▸ Splinter/tick forceps	1	Remove ticks
Personal health information form	1	Provide rescuers your key health information and contacts

Appendix C
SAMPLE WHISTLE PROTOCOL

A whistle is used to communicate to others in situations where human shouts cannot be heard and should be considered essential when hiking. Although three blasts on a whistle are recognized as HELP, there is no standardized response to let the initiator know they have been heard and response is on the way.

Colorado Mountain Club's Denver Safety and Leadership Committee (DS&L) developed a whistle protocol designed to be simple and effective for leaders and group members to initiate and respond in specific situations where the human voice may not be heard.

This matrix can be cut out and taped onto a water bottle with transparent tape, which helps protect the paper from moisture. In order to communicate in an emergency, *wear the whistle on the outside of the backpack or daypack.*

Recommended Whistle Protocol

Neither the initiator nor responder should cease whistle communication until the objective or the action requested is accomplished.

SITUATION/ OBJECTIVE	INITIATOR	RESPONSE
Contact	**1 Blast** *Where are you?*	**1 Blast** *I am here.*
Regroup	**2 Blasts** *Come here.*	**1 Blast** *Heard you. Coming.*
Emergency	**3 Blasts** *Help!*	**1 Blast** *Heard you. Coming.*

Recommended by CMC Denver Group Safety & Leadership Committee May 2015

Appendix D
LEAVE A TRACE TRIP PLAN

Hiker's name _____

Hiker's cell phone number _____

Is hiker carrying a personal locator beacon or satellite
communication device? (What type?) _____

_____

Vehicle: License, make, year, color _____

_____

Key clothing: Parka color, pack color, tent color _____

_____

Trail name_____

Trailhead location _____

Planned start date and time _____

Planned return date and time_____

Date and time when you should call for help _____

_____

Who to call, including phone number _____

_____

What to say: "I want to report a hiker who is overdue their planned return time. I was to be called if there was a delay. I have not heard from them."

In Colorado, county sheriffs have lead responsibility for all search and rescue (SAR). They may delegate activities to civilian SAR teams, who may call you for additional information. In national parks, rangers take the lead in SAR.

Appendix E

AVALANCHE FORECAST AND EDUCATION CENTERS

Avalanche centers provide current and predicted avalanche status reports. They are operated by the US Forest Service, state governments, and nonprofit organizations.

Forest Service Avalanche Centers

Bridgeport Avalanche Center
Bridgeport, CA; *bridgeportavalanchecenter.org*

Bridger-Teton Avalanche Center
Teton Village, WY; *jhavalanche.org*

Chugach National Forest Avalanche Center
Girdwood, AK; *cnfaic.org*

Flathead Avalanche Center
Hungry Horse, MT; *flatheadavalanche.org*

Gallatin National Forest Avalanche Center
Bozeman, MT; *mtavalanche.com*

Idaho Panhandle Avalanche Center
Ponderay, ID; *idahopanhandleavalanche.org*

National Avalanche Center
Bozeman, MT; *avalanche.org*

Northwest Avalanche Center
Seattle, WA; *nwac.us*

Mount Shasta Avalanche Center
Mount Shasta, CA; *shastaavalanche.org*

Mount Washington Avalanche Center
Gorham, NH; *mountwashingtonavalanchecenter.org*

Payette Avalanche Center
McCall, ID; *payetteavalanche.org*

Sawtooth Avalanche Center
Sun Valley, ID; *sawtoothavalanche.com*

Sierra Avalanche Center
Truckee, CA; *sierraavalanchecenter.org*

Utah Avalanche Center
Salt Lake City, UT; *utahavalanchecenter.org*

West Central Montana Avalanche Center
Missoula, MT; *missoulaavalanche.org*

State Avalanche Centers

Colorado Avalanche Information Center
Boulder, CO; *avalanche.state.co.us*

Local Nonprofit Avalanche Centers

Alaska Avalanche Information Center
(Nine locations in Alaska); *alaskasnow.org*

Central Oregon Avalanche Center
Bend, OR; *coavalanche.org*

Crested Butte Avalanche Center
Crested Butte, CO; *cbavalanchecenter.org*

Eastern Sierra Avalanche Center
Mammoth Lakes, CA; *esavalanche.org*

Hatcher Pass Avalanche Center
Palmer, AK; *hpavalanche.org*

Kachina Peaks Avalanche Center
Flagstaff, AZ; *kachinapeaks.org*

Wallowa Avalanche Center
Joseph, OR; *wallowaavalanchecenter.org*

GLOSSARY

acclimatization: Adjusting physiologically, over time, to increased altitude.

acute mountain sickness (AMS): The general term for altitude related illness caused by failure to acclimatize.

AFRCC: The United States Air Force Rescue Coordination Center.

alpine: Term used by naturalists to describe the high-altitude zone above tree line.

alpine start: An early-morning beginning of a hike, usually before sunrise.

animal trail (a.k.a. game trail): A trail created and used by animals, often without a clear beginning or end.

bearing: The compass direction from one spot to another measured from true north.

bergschrund: Crevasses located at the top of a snowfield or glacier where they have receded from cliff or snowfields above, dangerous for hikers to cross.

bivouac: A usually unplanned overnight camp, often uncomfortable and desperate. Hikers joke that the term *bivouac* is French for "mistake." The term is frequently shortened to "bivy."

bivy sack: A minimalist overnight shelter, usually a nylon sack.

BLM: Bureau of Land Management. The US government unit that manages certain federal lands, often remotely located.

blowdowns: Areas containing many fallen trees resulting from extremely high winds or microbursts. These often create very difficult travel when they straddle trails.

BLS: Basic life support. Skills used to provide emergency medicine.

boulder field: An area, often wide, of large stone boulders. These areas are typically on slopes, dangerous and difficult to cross.

braided river: River with numerous channels and often sand or gravel bars. These are often the best places to cross a wide river.

BSAR: Backcountry search and rescue is an essential service to search for, rescue, and sometimes recover deceased individuals from the backcountry.

bushwhacking: Commonly thought of as hiking off established trails, usually through dense vegetation. Also known as traveling cross-country.

cairn: A large pile of rocks used to mark the trail or cached items. Small rock piles are known as ducks.

CalTopo: A popular mapping software. It displays a set of digital maps to which a user can add location-based data. CalTopo originated with California maps, but now covers the entire United States and some foreign countries.

carabiner: Sturdy, oblong metal clip devices used in mountain climbing, useful for attaching ropes to fall-protection devices. Hikers use them for hanging bear bags and securely attaching gear to packs.

CDT: Continental Divide Trail.

Civil Air Patrol (CAP): Volunteer, auxiliary unit of the United States Air Force. These pilots, spotters, and support personnel search for lost aircraft and individuals.

confidence markers: Navigation markers placed along a trail to guide hikers. They are consistent symbols of uniform size or color. They are usually metal or plastic, nailed to trees or posts. They may also be rock piles or tree blazes. May be absent in federally designated wilderness areas.

contour lines: Colored lines on a topographic map, which indicate constant elevations.

contouring: Hiking along a slope and maintaining the same elevation.

cowboy camping: Purposely camping out without a tent or shelter.

CPR (cardio-pulmonary resuscitation): Emergency artificial respiration provided to stimulate heart and lung activity.

crampons: Metal spikes, strapped to boots to provide traction across ice or hard snow.

datum: Reference points used in creating maps. GPS devices use these points to orient the unit to a map.

declination: Adjustment of a compass to correct for differences between magnetic north and true north.

EMT: Emergency medical technician.

Esbit fuel: Fuel tablets used in ultralight backpacking stoves.

ETA: Estimated time of arrival.

exposure: 1) Older term for a medical condition we now more often describe as hypothermia. 2) Places on trails or cliff faces where a fall can cause injury or death.

fall line: The line of travel of a falling object, usually directly down a slope.

first lost point (FLP): Geographic location where a hiker first realizes they are lost. The FLP is a useful tool in becoming "unlost."

flash flood: Dangerous, rapid stream flooding resulting from intense rainfall. The rainfall may occur several miles upstream.

flip-flop: Consists of hiking a trail by starting at one end of the trail, hiking halfway, and returning to original starting point. Then travel to the trail end, hike to the midway point and return.

This allows for completely hiking a long trail and avoiding an overnight camp. It is also used by those without the ability to leave a vehicle or arrange a ride at the pickup point.

ford: Walking through water to cross a river or stream.

gaiters: Fabric sleeves, usually nylon, which are worn to cover the gap between boot top and pants cuff. Useful for keeping feet dry and pebbles from entering boots.

gear check: A quick break, early in a hike, to tighten pack straps, remove or add clothing layers, relace boots, and make sure all pockets are closed.

glissade: Controlled sliding on boots or pants bottom on snow, sand, or scree.

global positioning system (GPS): Navigation systems that use satellites to provide highly precise locations. Originally only operated by defense systems, they are now also placed by private enterprises.

graupel: Popcorn-like soft hail stones that may preceed cold fronts at higher altitudes. Pronounced "gropple."

HACE (high-altitude cerebral edema): A medical emergency when fluid collects in the brain due to increasing one's altitude without adequate acclimatization.

hasty team: A small, lightly equipped team of rescuers who are immediately dispatched to a backcountry incident. Their duties are to assess the situation, stabilize any patients, and advise the incident commanders of additional resource and evacuation needs.

HAPE (high-altitude pulmonary edema): A medical emergency where fluid fills alveolar spaces in the lungs due to increasing one's altitude without adequate acclimatization.

hypothermia: A dangerous, life-threatening condition due to lowered core body temperature.

ice axe: Pick-like tool mostly used by climbers for routes involving steep ice and snow. Hikers may carry as a safety device should their route take them into snowy territory.

incident command system (ICS): The organizational structure engaged to address large, complicated incidents. An ICS may coordinate the response to locating a lost hiker.

kicking steps: Occurs when hikers kick their boots into steep snow to create a foot base for climbing or ascending.

landing zone (LZ): This is the spot a rescue helicopter needs for landing. Usually, 100 square feet is considered the minimum space needed.

last known point (LNP): Location where a missing person was last known to be.

Leave No Trace (LNT): An educational program that promotes the sustainable use of wild lands. A nonprofit organization, the Leave No Trace Center for Outdoor Ethics, manages this national program. Conscientious hikers commit to Leave No Trace principles.

lollipop loop: A trail that starts and ends at the same point but in part encompasses a loop that is not repeated.

lost: Inability to know one's present location or reorient oneself to reach a known location.

magnetic declination: The difference between magnetic north and true north. It is expressed in degrees east or west of true north.

magnetic north: The point in the Artic to which needles of compasses are attracted. Magnetic north changes from time to time.

medivac: Word contraction for an emergency medical evacuation of a patient from a difficult, remote location. It involves a helicopter, litter team, or horses.

microfilter: Portable water filter that will remove bacteria, parasites, and protozoa from backcountry water sources.

microspikes: Spiked traction devices that attach to hiking shoes or boots. They are invaluable on icy trails and dirt roads. They are particularly helpful on late winter trails that have become compacted into "trenches."

MUDS: Hiker jargon for mindless ups and downs on a hike. (Also known as "PUDS" a.k.a. pointless ups and downs.)

near miss: An occurrence where the potential for a serious incident fortunately did not occur due to luck, a difference in timing, or a slight difference in location. Many more near misses occur than actual incidents.

NG911: Next generation 911 call software. Allows use of texting to reach 911 call centers.

NOAA SARSAT (National Oceanic and Atmospheric Administration Search and Rescue Satellite Aided Tracking): US government service that supports satellite enabled rescue tracking.

nobo: Hiking jargon for a northbound hiker.

NPS (National Park Service): Unit of the US Department of the Interior.

objective hazard: A physical hazard that may harm a hiker or climber. This may include exposure, rockslides, avalanches, flash floods, and so forth.

PLB (personal locator beacon): Electronic satellite device helpful for injured or ill hikers needing emergency evacuation.

PLS (place last seen): The location where a missing person was last seen. This may change as additional information comes to searchers.

PSAP (public safety answer points): The formal name for 911 call centers.

PSAR (preventative search and rescue): A concerted effort to educate and train the public about safe recreation behaviors in order to prevent the need for search and rescue assistance.

paramedic: An emergency medical technician who can provide sophisticated emergency medical care, including endotracheal intubation, starting IVs, and administering medication in prehospital care circumstances.

permanent snowfield: Snowfield that remains year-round but does not move, as a glacier may do.

posthole: Hole created in snow by hiker trekking through deep snow. Unpleasant and can be dangerous.

preheating: Forest fire behavior where burning spreads through creating heat, which dries out previously moist vegetation.

purifier filter: Water filter that removes bacteria, parasites, protozoa, and viruses.

rest step: A hiking step technique used for ascent in which each step ends with a temporary stop, resting on the skeletal structure. This provides a brief rest and allows for additional breaths as needed per step.

recovery position: The position an unconscious person should be placed in if a rescuer is unable to provide continuous attention. It involves moving a patient on their side so that their airway can remain open should they vomit or "swallow" their tongue. This method requires basic training acquired through a Wilderness First Aid course.

risk: The potential for something to turn out well or poorly. It is a concept that helps one cope with uncertainties in the environment.

risk literacy: The subjective ability to perceive risks in the environment and make appropriate decisions based on the level of that risk, also described as knowing what can go wrong.

risk management: The process of measuring risk and then developing and implementing strategies to reduce the impact of unfortunate events or maximize the realization of positive opportunities.

scrambling: Off-trail travel on steep terrain that may require the use of hands. Ropes are not normally used in scrambling.

scree: Small, loose rocks that are smaller than talus and boulders.

search and rescue (SAR): Organized efforts to find lost or injured individuals, stabilize, and evacuate them to safety.

snowpack telemetry (SNOTEL): Remote, backcountry weather stations that measure snow accumulation. There are 730 sites located in the American West.

sobo: Hiker jargon for south-bound hiker.

surveyors tape: Brightly colored plastic tape, usually 1-inch wide. It is a highly useful safety tool used to mark trail junctions or routes through dense vegetation.

talus: Rock fragments, often sharp, that are big enough to step on individually.

terminus: The end point of a trail.

thru-hiker: A person who hikes a long-distance trail from one end to the other.

topos: Topographical maps, which show elevation and contours. Very useful for hikers.

trail angels: Kind individuals who provide hikers with water, soda, snacks, a place to stay, and rides to and from the trail to civilization.

trail name: Nickname given to hikers by other hikers. Common practice on long-distance trails.

tree line: Area at high altitude above which trees cannot grow.

true north: The geographic North Pole. Most maps are designed oriented to true north.

UIAA (International Climbing and Mountaineering Federation): International organization, based in Switzerland, that sets climbing equipment standards. In recent years, they are moving toward creating a range of standards for guides and educators.

ultralight hiker: A backpacker who strives to lower their pack weight as much as possible, sometimes to twelve pounds or less. These hikers need to be skilled, experienced, and highly self-reliant, as limited equipment may increase hazard issues.

USAR (urban search and rescue): This form of rescue usually involves assisting individuals trapped in collapsed buildings.

verglas: Dangerous, clear ice coating that adheres to rock. Falls are possible and can be deadly if exposure is involved.

wilderness: An area of land largely undisturbed by humankind. Such areas typically lack roads and human development. The US Congress defines wilderness as "an area where the earth and its community of life are untrammeled by man, where man himself is a visitor who does not remain." There are

756 US federally designated wilderness areas, and they are found in all fifty states. In this book, "wilderness" is used synonymously with "backcountry" and "outback."

Wilderness First Aid (WFA): Initial care provided for acute illness or injury occurring in a wilderness setting. Wilderness for first aid purposes has been defined as being in a remote location more than one hour from definitive medical care.

Wilderness First Responder (WFR): An individual trained to respond to emergency incidents in remote locations. It is considered the gold standard in Wilderness First Aid training.

Wilderness Risk Management Conference (WRMC): An annual, educational conference that is "ground zero" for the latest in risk-management education. Hosted by the National Outdoor Leadership School, Outward Bound, and the Student Conservation Association.

SOURCES AND RECOMMENDED READING

Introduction

Berman, Joshua. "The Surge." *Elevation Outdoors*. Spring 2022.

Blevins, Jason. "Colorado's Volunteer Search and Rescue Teams Are Overwhelmed and There Are Fears It's Going to Get Worse." *Colorado Sun*. March 31, 2020.

Colorado Parks and Wildlife. "Backcountry Search and Rescue Study." State of Colorado. January 17, 2022.

Chapter 1: The Meaning of Safety

Abbey, Edward. *Desert Solitaire*. New York: Simon and Shuster, 1968, 169.

Deeter, Michael. "The Psychology of Bad Decision Making." *Wilderness Medicine Magazine* 37, no. 2. May 25, 2020.

Ettinger, Stephan, et al. "Search and Rescue in the Pacific West States." *Wilderness Environmental Medicine* 33, no. 1 (2022): 41–49.

Funderburke, Ron. "Speak Up: Intervening Effectively for Safer Climbing." *North American Climbing*. 2019.

Gladbach, Steve. Steve Gladbach Memorial Moments Educational Videos. YouTube. youtube.com/playlist?app=desktop&list=PLDFGmYrMwb6DAolOimsjhdmkFronyyjy9.

Harvey, Mark. *The National Outdoor Leadership School's Wilderness Guide.* New York: Fireside, 1999, 24.

Kosseff, Alex. *AMC Guide to Outdoor Leadership.* Boston: Appalachian Mountain Club Books, 2003.

Leemon, Drew, Katie Mettenbrink, and Tod Schimelpfeng. *Risk Management for Outdoor Leaders.* 2nd ed. Lander, WY: National Outdoor Leadership School, 2019.

McGladrey, Laura. "It Doesn't Just Happen: Applying Intention, Best Practice, and Lessons Learned Around Occupational Stress to the Future of Risk Management in the Outdoor Industry." Wilderness Risk Management Conference—Facing Challenges Together. October 18, 2021.

Peruzzi, Marc. "Why 'the Withdrawal' Makes Sense to Outdoor Athletes." *Elevation Outdoors*. October 29, 2021. elevationoutdoors.com/magazine/october-november-2021/why-the-withdrawal-makes-sense-to-outdoor-athletes/

Rafferty, Dan. "Risk Assessment for the Colorado Mountain Club." University of Colorado Denver: Spring Semester 2021.

Scott-Nash, Mark. *Colorado 14er Disasters.* 2nd ed. Golden, CO: Colorado Mountain Club Press, 2016.

Smith, Steve, ed. *Beneficial Risks: The Evolution of Risk Management for Outdoor and Experiential Education Programs*. Champaign, IL: Sagamore Venture, 2021.

Stott, Sandy. "Accidents." *Appalachia.* Winter/Spring 2022.

Zachary, N. Lu, Amy Briggs, Soheil Saadat, and Isabel Algaze. "The Associations Between Visitation, Social Media Use and Search and Rescue in United States National Parks." *Wilderness & Environmental Medicine 32*, no. 4. December 2021.

Chapter 2: Clothing

Helmuth, Diana. *How to Suffer Outside: A Beginners Guide to Hiking and Backpacking.* Seattle: Mountaineers Books, 2021.

Long, John. *The Little Book of Outdoor Wisdom.* Lanham, MD: Falcon Guides, 2019.

REI.com. "Layering Basics." Expert Advice. 2022.

Chapter 3: Water Hazards

Blehm, Eric. *The Last Season.* New York: Harper-Collins, 2009.

Evergreen Parks and Recreation District. "Ice Safety." Evergreen, CO. 2020.

Fredston, Jill, and Doug Feste. *Snow Sense: A Guide to Evaluating Snow Avalanche Hazard.* Anchorage: Alaska Mountain Safety Center, 2011.

McKee, Spencer. "Colorado Asks: Is That Ice Thick Enough to Hold My Weight?" Out There Colorado. December 21, 2021. outtherecolorado.com/adventures/colorado-asks-is-that-ice-thick-enough-to-hold-my-weight/article_fda12c3a-6286-11ec-bc3a-37bedc2c9387.html.

Ostis, Nate. *River Rescue.* Mechanicsburg, PA: Stackpole Books, 2010.

———. *NOLS River Rescue Guide.* Mechanicsburg, PA: Stackpole Books, 2015.

Stott, Sandy, ed. "Accidents." *Appalachia.* Winter/Spring 2019.

Chapter 4: Weather

Christie, Tim. "Weather That Kills." *Colorado Outdoors.* January/February 2021.

Cordes, Ron. *Pocket Guide to Weather Forecasting.* Austin, TX: Pocket Guides Publishing, 2014.

Day, John A., and Vincent J. Schaefer. *Peterson's First Guide to Clouds and Weather.* Boston: Houghton Mifflin, 1991.

Densmore, Lisa. "Master Class: Predict the Weather." *Backpacker.* September 2014, 40.

Harvey, Mark. *The National Outdoor Leadership School Wilderness Guide.* New York: Simon and Schuster, 1999.

Leipold, Catherina. "Predict the Weather." *Backpacker.* September 2015.

National Weather Service. "User-Defined Forecast Website Tutorial." Grand Junction, CO. 2022. weather.gov.

Powers, Phil. *Wilderness Mountaineering.* Mechanicsburg, PA: Stackpole Books, 1993.

Schimelpfenig, Tod, and Paggett, Justin. *Wilderness Medicine Field Guide.* 5th ed. Lander, WY: National Outdoor Leadership School, 2016.

Zafren, Ken, Gordon G. Giesbrecht, Daniel F. Danzl, Hermann Brugger, Emily B. Sagalyn, Beat Walpoth, Eric A. Weiss, Paul S. Auerbach, Scott E. McIntosh, Mária Némethy, Marion McDevitt, Jennifer Dow, Robert B. Schoene, George W. Rodway, Peter H. Hackett, Brad L. Bennett, and Colin K. Grissom. "Wilderness Medicine Society Practice Guidelines for the Out-of-Hospital Evaluation of and Treatment of Accidental Hypothermia." *Wilderness Environmental Medicine* 24, no. 4 (2014): 586–595.

Chapter 5: Lightning

Beckmann, Bruce. "Lightning Awareness." Alpine Rescue Team. alpinerescueteam.org/safety-education/lightning-awareness/.

Cherim, Mike. "Travel Etiquette 201: A New Code for a Complicated Era." *Appalachia.* Summer/Fall 2002.

Cooper, Mary Ann, Ronald L. Holle, and Christopher J. Andrews. "Distribution of Lightning Injury Mechanisms." Preprints, Proceeding's 20th International Lightning Detection Conference. Tucson, AZ: Vaisala, 2008.

Ferstle, Jim. "The Lowdown on Lightning." *Backpacker*. July 1986.

Gookin, John. *Lightning*. Mechanicsburg, PA: Stackpole Books, 2014.

Heilkamp, Todd, Al Ossinger, and Wayne Ruff. *Lightning in the Mountains: How to Avoid Lightning Accidents*. Golden, CO: Colorado Mountain Club Foundation.

Holle, Ronald L. "Lightning Fatalities Weighted by Population by State." Tucson, AZ: Vaisala, 2018.

NOAA. "What Causes Lightning and Thunder?" scijinks.gov/lightning/.

Schimelpfenig, Tod. *NOLS Wilderness Medicine*. 7th ed. Lanham, MD: Stackpole Books, 2021.

Stewart, Donna. "Lightning Strikes." *Elevation Outdoors*. June 2019.

Walher, Matt. "Dress for Lighting." *Backpacker*. October 2011.

Chapter 6: Terrain and Pace

Bukay, Corey. "Cliffed Out." *Backpacker*. May/June 2021, 35.

Fletcher, Colin, and Chip Rawlins. *The Complete Walker IV*. New York: Alfred A. Knopf, 2002.

Gookin, John, and Adam Swisher, eds. *NOLS Wilderness Education Notebook*. 11th ed. Lander, WY: National Outdoor Leadership School, 2015.

Heid, Matt. "Need Advice on Trekking Poles? Follow This Way." *AMC Outdoors*. Spring 2018, 16–17.

Linxweiler, Eric, and Mike Maude, eds. *Mountaineering: The Freedom of the Hills*. 9th ed. Seattle: Mountaineers Books, 1992.

Silva, Kaelyn. "Next Level: The Rest Step." *Backpacker*. April 9, 2008. backpacker.com/skills/next-level-the-rest-step/.

Song, Michelle. "Learning from Near-Misses." *Mountaineer Magazine.* Fall 2021.

Tsuboi, Tony. "Outside Insights/Active Terrain Management." *Mountaineer Magazine*. Spring 2021.

Chapter 7: Altitude

Auerbach, Paul. *Medicine for the Outdoors.* 5th ed. Philadelphia: Mosby-Elsevier, 2009.

Bezruchka, Stephan. *Altitude Illness Prevention and Treatment.* 2nd ed. Seattle: Mountaineers Books, 2005.

Lentz, Martha. *Mountaineering First Aid.* 5th ed. Seattle: Mountaineers Books, 2004.

Lovette, Richard. "Two Weeks in the Mountains Can Change Your Blood for Months." *Science.* October 2016. science.org/content/article/two-weeks-mountains-can-change-your-blood-months#:~:text=The%20most%20recent%20finding%3A%20Even,after%20descending%20to%20lower%20elevations.

Luks, Andrew M., Paul S. Auerbach, Luanne Freer, Colin K. Grissom, Linda E. Keyes, Scott E. McIntosh, George W. Rodway, Robert B. Schoene, Ken Zafren, and Peter H. Hackett. "Wilderness Medical Society Practice Guidelines for the Prevention and Treatment of Acute Altitude Illness: 2019 Update." *Wilderness Environmental Medicine* 4S (2019): S3–S18.

Weber, Dave. "High Altitude Illness Prevention, Assessment, and Treatment." *Accidents in North American Climbing* II, no 1, 36–37.

Winger, Charlie, and Diane Winger. *Highpoint Adventures*. Littleton, CO: Sequoia Publishing, 1999.

Zyzda, Mike. "It Can Happen to You! A Climbers Experience with HAPE." *Trail and Timberline.* Summer 2017, 32–33.

Chapter 8: The Ten Essentials

Giordano, Claire. "What's Your Eleventh Essential? Celebrating the Ten Essentials." *Mountaineer Magazine*. Spring 2021.

Mountaineers, The. "The Ten Essentials—A Systems Approach." mountaineers.org/locations-lodges/tacoma-branch/committees/tacoma-hiking-backpacking-committee/hike-leader-resources/the-10-essentials.

Mountaineers, The. "What Are the Ten Essentials?" October 20, 2020. mountaineers.org/blog/what-are-the-ten-essentials.

Ramsey, Sarah. "The Day Hiker's Ten Essentials." March 3, 2018. mountaineers.org/blog/the-day-hikers-ten-essentials.

Chapter 9: Staying Found *and* Chapter 10: Lost

Christie, Tim. "Lost." *Colorado Outdoors Hunting Guide*. Colorado Department of Parks and Wildlife, 2020.

Congressional Research Service. "Wildfire Statistics." September 2, 2022. sgp.fas.org/crs/misc/IF10244.pdf.

Gonzales, Laurence. *Deep Survival: Who Lives, Who Dies, and Why*. New York: Norton, 2003.

Griffith, Joe. "Follow That Trail: Tools for Navigating Your Next Hike." *Trail and Timberline*. Spring 2015.

Hill, Kenneth. *Lost Person Behavior: The Psychology of Lost.* Ottawa, ONT: National SAR Secretariate, 1998.

Koester, Robert. *Lost Person Behavior*. Charlottesville, VA: DBS Productions, 2008.

Reppenhagen, Cory. "More Wildfires Start on July 4 Than Any Other Day of the Year." 9News. July 2, 2020. 9news.com/article/weather/weather-colorado/more-wildfires-start-on-july-4-than-any-other-day/73-55957e6d-74cf-4477-b03f-a4b671aad75b.

Syrotuck, William. *Analysis of Lost Person Behavior.* Mechanicsburg, PA: Barkleigh Productions, 2012.

Chapter 11: Forest Fires

Brennan, Charlie. "CU Researcher Tracks Fire-Starting 'Switches.'" *Denver Post.* June 12, 2018.

Christiansen, Vicki. "Collaboration Across Boundaries: A Policy Perspective on the State of Wildland Fire." Speech presented at the Wildland-Urban Interface Conference. Reno, NV. February 2018.

Pacific Crest Trail Association. "How to React to Wildfires." 2019. pcta.org/discover-the-trail/backcountry-basics/fire/how-to-react-to-wildfires/.

KTVQ News. "Ominous Trend in American West Could Signal a Looming 'Megadrought.'" May 9, 2020. youtube.com/watch?v=TJAHNb6hoec.

Tilton, Morgan. "In the Black." *Elevation Outdoors.* March 2019.

USDA Forest Service. "InciWeb—Incidental Information System." inciweb.nwcg.gov.

USDA Forest Service. *"Active Fire Mapping Program."* Remote Sensing Application Center. fsapps.nwegov/atm.

USDA Forest Service. "*Outdoor Fire Safety.*" December 1990.

Chapter 12: Animal Encounters

Alvarez, Ted. "The Truth About Bears." *Backpacker.* March 2013.

Boulder County Sheriff's Office, Animal Control Unit. "Do You Know Which Snake Is a Rattlesnake?" Boulder, CO. 2020.

Center for Wildlife Information. "Bear Pepper Spray, What Retailers and Consumers Should Know About Pepper Spray." Missoula, MT. 2007.

Childs, Craig. *The Animal Dialogues.* New York: Back Bay Books, 2007.

Colorado Parks and Wildlife. "Living With Coyotes, How to Avoid Wildlife Contacts." Denver, CO. June 2014.

Colorado Parks and Wildlife. "Living with Lions." Denver, CO. March 2011.

Colorado Parks and Wildlife. "Living with Wildlife in Moose Country." Denver, CO. March 2011.

Den Mother. "What Should I Do About a Snake Bite?" *Backpacker*. May 11, 2015.

Dinets, Vladimir. *Peterson Field Guide to Finding Mammals in North America*. New York: Houghton Mifflin, 2015.

Heil, Nick. "Shoot or Spray? The Best Way to Stop a Bear." *Outside*. May 2012. outsideonline.com/1899301/shoot-or-spray-best-way-stop-charging-bear/.

Lofholm, Nancy. "Anxious Trails, Large Guard Dogs Tending Sheep Frighten Hikers in the Backcountry." *Denver Post*. August 24, 2014.

McIntyre, Rich. *The Rise of Wolf 8*. Vancouver, BC: Greystone, 2019.

McKee, Spencer. "Are Wolves a Threat to Colorado Hikers?" *Out There Colorado*. January 16, 2020.

Mitchel, Kirk. "Colorado Trail Runner Attacked by Mountain Lion, Choked Cat to Death with Hands, Arms and Feet." *Denver Post*. February 5, 2019.

Montana Fish, Wildlife, and Parks. "Wolves and Human Safety." fwp.mt.gov/fishandwildlife/management/wolf/human.html.

National Park Service: Grand Teton National Park. "Carry Bear Spray — Know How to Use It." nps.gov/grte/planyourvisit/bear_spray.htm.

Schneider, Bill. *Bear Aware*. 2nd ed. Guilford, CT: Falcon Guides, 2001.

Smith, Dave. *Don't Get Eaten, The Danger of Animals that Charge or Attack*. Seattle: Mountaineers Books, 2003.

Smith, Douglas, and Gary Ferguson. *Decade of the Wolf, Returning the Wild to Yellowstone*. Guilford, CT: Lyons Press, 2012.

Smith, Logan. "Wild Pigs in Colorado? Not Anymore, Say Wildlife Officials." CBS Denver. February 15, 2020.

Wickstrom, Terry. "Tips to Avoid Lion Attacks." *Denver Post*. February 15, 2017.

Wickstrom, Terry. "What to Do if You Came Across a Moose, Fawn and Coyotes in the Colorado Outdoors?" *Denver Post*. January 18, 2018.

Wikihow. "How to Survive a Wolf Attack." December 16, 2020. wikihow.com/Survive-a-Wolf-Attack/

Wilson, Dawn. "Moose on the Move." *Colorado Outdoors*. September/October 2019.

Wysocki, Annette, and Laurance Wiland. "The Striking Truth About Snakes." *Backpacker*. May 1992.

Chapter 13: Communication Safety Tools

Lambe, Dick. "Signaling for Help by Satellite." *The Mountaineer*. September/October 2005, 30–31.

Nair, Tim. "Connections in the Sky: Mountaintop Ham Radio." *The Mountaineer*. September/October 2015.

"Safety, Guides Are Careful." *Backpacker*. August 2017, 80.

Schwartz, Jason. "Saved by the Cell Phone." *Backpacker*. September 2015.

Scott-Nash, Mark. *Colorado 14er Disasters*. 2nd ed. Golden, CO: Colorado Mountain Club Press, 2016.

Wichelns, Ryan. "Everything You Need to Know About Personal Locator Beacons and Satellite Communications." REI. December 2021.

Chapter 14: Backcountry Street Smarts

Andrews, Steve. "An Ode to Solo Backcountry Travel and a Theory on How to Make It Safer." The Inertia, December 21, 2021. theinertia.com/mountain/an-ode-to-solo-backcountry-travel-and-a-theory-on-how-to-make-it-safer/.

Arvesen, Amelia. "How to Face Your Fear of Backpacking Alone." May 11, 2021. backpacker.com/skills/how-to-face-your-fear-of-backpacking-alone/.

Orsi, Gabrielle. "How to: Deal with a Smash and Grab." The Mountaineers Blog. February 27, 2019.

Paul, Susan Joy. *Women in the World.* Guilford, CT: Falcon Guides, 2021.

Stott, Sandy. "Accidents." *Appalachia.* Winter/Spring 2019.

USDA Forest Service. "Crime Prevention." usda.gov/visit/know-before-you-go/crime-prevention.

Wohlleben, Peta. *The Heartbeat of Trees: Embracing Our Ancient Bond with Forests and Nature.* London, UK: Harper Collins, 2021.

Young, Mark. "Trail Safety: The Perception and Reality." *Deportment.* July 1, 2014

ABOUT THE AUTHOR

Photo by Ellen Nelson

If something unexpected or dangerous can occur in the back-country, **ART HOGLING** has experienced it and is surprised he survived it. In his decades of wilderness hiking and climbing around the world, he has been attacked by predators, confronted two-legged dangers, experienced the fear of being lost, and been caught in lightning storms, blizzards, forest fires, avalanches, and flash floods. Dr. Hogling has embraced and learned from it all, combining it with technical research to produce popular hiking safety classes and curriculums.

Art has taught wilderness safety for over twenty-five years, is a Wilderness First Responder, Certified First Aid Instructor, Master Wilderness Safety Instructor, and a member of the Wilderness Medical Society. He co-founded and is current director of the Colorado Mountain Club Hiking Safety Seminars. Art is a retired health care administrator. He continues to teach university graduate courses. Art lives in the mountains of Colorado.

Illustration by Jesse Crock

Join Today.
Adventure Tomorrow.

The Colorado Mountain Club is the Rocky Mountain community for mountain education, adventure, and conservation. We bring people together to share our love of the mountains. We value our community and go out of our way to welcome and include all Coloradoans—from the uninitiated to the expert, there is a place for everyone here.

cmc.org